LIVING FEARLESS IN CHRIST

Why I Left Islam to Win Battles for the Kingdom

BY

HEDIEH MIRAHMADI FALCO

LIVING FEARLESS IN CHRIST
Why I Left Islam to Win Battles for the Kingdom

MIRAHMADI FALCO, HEDIEH, Author
LIVING FEARLESS IN CHRIST
HEDIEH MIRAHMADI FALCO

Resurrect Ministry
30700 Russell Ranch Road Ste 250
Westlake Village, CA 91362
ResurrectMinistry.com

In Association With:
ELITE ONLINE PUBLISHING
63 East 11400 South Suite 230
Sandy, UT 84070
EliteOnlinePublishing.com

ISBN - 978-1-961801-40-0 (Paperback)
ISBN - 978-1-961801-42-4 (Audiobook)
ISBN - 978-1-961801-41-7 (eBook)

REL012120
REL012170
BIO018000

QUANTITY PURCHASES: Schools, companies, professional groups,
clubs, and other organizations may qualify for special terms
when ordering quantities of this title.
For information, email info@resurrectministry.com.

TABLE OF CONTENTS

FOREWORD

As someone who has witnessed the effects of God's grace on a tired and restless soul, and His power to transform a willing vessel, I have had the joy of seeing this first-hand in the life of Hedieh Mirahmadi Falco. Knowing Hedieh personally and that she was writing this book, I have anticipated the honor of writing this foreword. I can't wait to see what God will do in the lives of those who read *"Living Fearless in Christ."*

Hedieh is a remarkable woman of deep faith, courage, and compassion, whose journey has not been without its trials. As a former devout Muslim, her path to Christianity was fraught with challenges that required immense bravery. Yet, through it all, she has never wavered in her trust in Jesus Christ, demonstrating a resilience and strength that are truly inspiring.

As a first-generation Persian-American with roots in Iran, Hedieh believed her destiny and religious heritage were realized in Islam. Fast forward: Hedieh earned a doctorate in law from USC and bachelor's degree from UCLA living in Beverly Hills, California. Seeing the flaws and dangers of radical Islam and its negative impact on culture, she spent two decades as a counterterrorism expert, working with foreign governments, the U.S. government, and the FBI against Al Qaeda and ISIS. In 2006, while pregnant, Hedieh escaped war-torn Lebanon by hiding in the trunk of a friend's car and eventually made her way back to the United States.

Hedieh honestly and bravely discovered that after twenty-four years of practicing Islam, she was (in her own words), "Living in a relationship with a dead god, a false god, where there was no real life nor an answer for my sins and my quest for meaning." — That is until she met Jesus! While watching a sermon on a YouTube channel, she experienced a personal encounter with Jesus Christ.

Hedieh invites us to walk alongside her as she navigates the complexities of leaving Islam, embracing a new faith, and establishing her identity in Christ. Her story is not only one of religious conversion but also a testament to the transformative power of God's love — a love that heals, redeems, and empowers. Perhaps you've felt something similar, whether it's Islam, Mormonism, atheism, or another belief that has left you feeling unsure, disillusioned, and empty.

In *"Living Fearless in Christ"* Hedieh shares her experiences with remarkable personal honesty and vulnerability, which I truly appreciate, as so few people are willing to be seen through such a lens. I can attest to the fact that Hedieh's unwavering commitment to her faith and her passion for sharing the Gospel shine through all that she does. Whether in ministry with her husband or her commitment to counsel families struggling with loved ones bound by the shackles of Islam, she speaks with authority as one who has walked through the fire and emerged refined, not weakened. Her experiences, from childhood trauma to an impressive career combating Islamic extremism, have shaped her into a fearless warrior for Christ.

I believe this book will resonate with many. It offers hope to the struggling, encouragement to the weary, and inspiration to those seeking a deeper relationship with the one true God through our Lord Jesus Christ. Hedieh's story is a powerful reminder that God is always with us, even in the darkest times, and that His love can overcome any obstacle.

Jack Hibbs
Pastor, Calvary Chapel Chino Hills & President, Real Life Network

PROLOGUE

The 2024 US elections were a decisive victory for conservative and Christian principles, a landmark moment that rekindled hope in the hearts of many Americans. This resounding triumph signifies a renewed embrace of traditional values, signaling a profound desire for positive change in the direction of our nation. Emboldened by this outcome, we optimistically anticipate that America will embark on a transformative journey, repudiating its past missteps and transgressions.

As we move forward, this triumph should be a clarion call to restore justice and human dignity as the cornerstone of our government policies. We are at a pivotal moment in American history. The majority of the country wants to turn the corner–a collective decision to embrace our values and work towards a brighter future for ourselves and generations to come. Having won all three branches of power, it is a clear mandate from the American people that they care more about the rising costs of food and the dangerous rise of migrant crime than boys playing in girl's sports. However, let us not forget that the victory has left our nation deeply divided, with a sense of both relief and uncertainty hanging in the balance. We do not know the outcome of this battle as it plays out in cities across America, so my desire to raise awareness of the issues contained in this book is as important as ever.

The road ahead will not be easy. The defeated left is already mobilizing resistance, and we must be prepared to respond with patience, truth, and grace. This is not the time for Christians to rely on the government to fight our battles for us; that is what led us to this precarious position in the first place. Instead, we must actively engage in the political process, advocating for policies that align with our values and seeking to build bridges across the divide. I firmly believe that while millions of Americans may not have voted for Trump, we can all find common ground—especially within the Church, where we share in the ministry of reconciliation. It will require compromise and compassion on both sides.

While many celebrate the defeat of a radical progressive agenda, we must not fall into complacency or political idolatry. As people of faith, we are called to be watchmen on the wall, upholding Biblical values and warning of dangers others may not see or that they choose to ignore. We must also use our discernment not to blindly accept changes that can have negative, unintended consequences.

As an example, let us thoughtfully consider the issue of returning prayer and Biblical teaching to public schools. Like millions of Christians across the nation, I was excited to hear Trump announce it would be part of his national agenda. It was a breath of fresh air to hear respect and support for the values that form the bedrock of our nation. However, as someone who has directly participated in well-meaning government programs that go terribly wrong, I have a sense of trepidation about how exactly that would be executed. We must never forget that our founding fathers escaped the state-run Church in Europe to practice religion freely. There is a delicate balance that must be struck between support for religious freedom and violating the constitutional limits placed on choosing one religion over another. Though it may be encouraging for Christians now, imagine a scenario where we have a Catholic president, and the prayer is changed to the rosary. Would Protestant Christians be as accepting of that?

It is also encouraging that the new administration champions a foreign policy that decreases U.S. support for foreign wars. Trump's endorsement of the Reagan doctrine—peace through strength—translates into a strong U.S. military while decreasing our financial support of endless overseas conflicts. This means defending religious liberty and freedom of expression while also promoting a common-sense approach to foreign policy that prioritizes peace and avoids endless wars.

Above all, we must remember that the Gospel spread throughout Asia long before the Church held any political power. Our strength lies not in worldly influence but in our unwavering commitment to the truth and our willingness to love our neighbors as ourselves. Let us move forward with humility, wisdom, and courage, trusting in God's guidance as we navigate the challenges ahead.

In the words of the Apostle Paul, let us *"make every effort to do what leads to peace and mutual edification."* Only then can we hope to heal the wounds of this divisive election and build a more just and compassionate society for all.

ABOUT THE COVER

In the Bible, in the book of Revelation, Chapter 4, verses 2-8, it reads in part:

"At once I was in the Spirit, and there before me was a throne in Heaven with someone sitting on it. And the one who sat there had the appearance of jasper and ruby. A rainbow that shone like an emerald encircled the throne. Surrounding the throne were twenty-four other thrones, and seated on them were twenty-four elders. They were dressed in white and had crowns of gold on their heads. From the throne came flashes of lightning, rumblings and peals of thunder. In front of the throne, seven lamps were blazing. These are the seven spirits of God. Also, in front of the throne there was what looked like a sea of glass, clear as crystal.

In the center, around the throne, were four living creatures, and they were covered with eyes, in front and in back. The first living creature was like a lion, the second was like an ox, the third had a face like a man, the fourth was like a flying eagle. Each of the four living creatures had six wings and was covered with eyes all around, even under its wings. Day and night they never stop saying:

'Holy, holy, holy
is the Lord God Almighty,
who was, and is, and is to come.'"

This passage describes a vision of the apostle John, who saw four living creatures symbolizing the faithful ministers of the Gospel standing between the throne and the elders. Some say that the four living creatures symbolize the various gifts that God bestows upon His ministers. These gifts include courage and fortitude (lion), mildness and meekness (ox or calf), wisdom and prudence (man), and piercing insight into the mysteries of God's Kingdom (eagle).

Most importantly, their primary function is worship. Day and night, they never stop singing praises to God. Over and over again, they say, "Holy, Holy, Holy." It signifies how God has worked in our past, how He works in our present, and how He will work in our future. They sit in the throne room of God and sing His praises without ceasing. The 24 elders fall down at the sound and passion of these four living creatures, acknowledging their insight and wisdom in worship of the Lord, the one who sits on the throne.

Worship plays an important role in God's Kingdom. We worship God because of His greatness and for the wondrous deeds He has done. These creatures serve as a visible reminder of the majesty and glory of God and His abiding presence with His people. They also teach us that God infuses several aspects of Himself into His creation. Humans may be the only ones made "in His image," but other creations show His traits. In the four living creatures, we see signs of God's divine power, patience, wisdom, and dominion.

Knowing that God's traits are reflected in what He creates, we should look for those reflections in the world around us—in nature and people. For example, we may know someone who displays God's mercy or sense of justice more than we do. We should delight in seeing God's characteristics in ourselves and our world.

The role of these four creatures continues when Jesus appears on the scene in Heaven in Revelation 5 and they are each holding golden bowls full of incense, which are the prayers of God's people. They are holding our prayers.

"And they sang a new song, saying:

You are worthy to take the scroll and to open its seals, because you were slain, and with your blood you purchased for God persons from every tribe and language and people and nation. You have made them to be a Kingdom and priests to serve our God, and they will reign on the earth." —Rev 5: 9-10

They interpret what John is witnessing, telling us who we are and what we represent in this world and the next. It wasn't just a vision for John. It was for us. The four living creatures are telling us "be holy". Jesus' blood redeemed you and made you a Kingdom and priesthood. You are worshippers of the Father and it is by the Lamb you are given eternal life to live and to reign with Him forever.

These words have carried me through the most challenging times in my walk with Jesus. The Holy Spirit calls my heart back to the holiness of God so I can find peace in His presence. When the publishers and I opened a contest for the cover design, the Lord made it clear to my heart it must be the four living creatures.

INTRODUCTION

"You are sons of Light, daughters of Day….let's not sleepwalk through life like those others. Let's keep our eyes open and be smart. People sleep at night and get drunk at night. But not us! Since we're creatures of Day, let's act like it. Walk out into the daylight sober, dressed up in faith, love, and the hope of salvation."

—*1 Thessalonians 5:5 MSG*

I am acutely aware that no one escapes this life without trials, tribulations, and sometimes a very healthy dose of drawbacks. *No one.*

There's no denying the vast differences between each of our struggles. I definitely was not the most abused person on the planet, but I've been around the block a *whole* lot of times. I know what I've had to overcome in my life is *enormous.*

I'm not boasting. I am simply trying to present an accurate picture of who I am and how I got here.

I would describe myself as a *warrior.*

Why? If I truly wanted to live up to my God-given potential in the Kingdom of Christ, I had to achieve victory in all the major battlegrounds of life. First, I needed to pick up the shattered pieces of myself and find wholeness in my new relationship with the Risen Savior. Second, it was establishing my own identity in a new religion. The customs, the people, even the food was different! All of this came with navigating who I was to be as a mother and stay-at-home wife to a brand-new family. I had no point of reference for the duties and responsibilities of a household other than what I witnessed in the sweet example of my mother. Though this would have been enough for most people, I was soon called to use my professional experience and new faith to fight for the societal values and political future I wanted for my community and my country. "Battle-tested and combat-ready," the Lord said. Even just one of those on its own can be challenging, if not blisteringly tough. All five simultaneously felt *apocalyptic*.

The most daunting thing I had to do to become a warrior for Christ was to leave Islam. Any of you who have tried to leave the religion with which you have affiliated for most of your life know how difficult—and sometimes even dangerous—that can be. You also know that you're not the only one on the voyage. Many others in your life go along for the ride, often unwillingly. Your decision affects your entire family, your companion, your children, your employer, and your friends, and they, too, can be subjected to the same difficulty and danger you are.

I knew all that even before I started on my journey. I also knew that I had to establish a relationship with Jesus Christ that would stop addictions, heal all aspects of myself, and break the generational curses that were holding me back.

I had to pursue holiness with everything I had.

I believe that writing this book is more than fulfilling my own calling. As far back as I know, I am the first believer in Christ in my bloodline. My conversion is a legacy that I leave not only for my daughter but for her children and her children's children. I pray that it breaks the generational curses I suffered through and gives future generations a chance to live a life filled with unconditional love and faith.

I also pray that it breaks the strongholds in YOUR life. I pray you find encouragement and strength in my calling so YOU become a warrior alongside me. Whether you are a Pakistani Muslim immigrant or a native-born American raised in the church but far from God, I wrote this book for YOU. I sincerely pray that as you read these words, including most powerfully the Scripture I have included, you will initiate your personal relationship with the Savior of all Mankind, Jesus Christ. May the Lord's words inspire you to be bold and courageous.

I dedicate this book to my amazing husband, Andy, and my precious daughter, Zahra, who has endured so much suffering to walk this journey with me. Andy is the most supportive and encouraging man I have ever met. She and I are so blessed to have him as the leader of our household. I am also eternally grateful to the Kingdom saints who taught me and prayed for me to become the believer I am today. To the great men of God, Pastor Jack Hibbs and Pastor Bob Kopeny, who feed me the meat of the word. May the Lord bless you endlessly for what you do.

Finally, we can never give up until the Lord calls us home. Despite the darkness, we are people of the Light.

— PART 1 —

TRANSFORMING
SELF

"There is a God-shaped vacuum in the heart of every man which cannot be filled by any created thing, but only by God, the Creator, made known through Jesus."

~ Blaise Pascal

ONE

Living Fast and Furious

"When you walk through the fire, you will not be scorched, nor will the flame burn you."

—Isaiah 43:2

The American Dream inspired my parents to move to the United States in 1967. It was long before the Islamic revolution, so they were excited to start a new life in a country that they knew was filled with opportunities. I was born in Chicago after their arrival, while my father finished his medical training and my mother worked as a manicurist to pay the bills. They sought freedom, greater wealth, unbridled opportunity, and the promise of a better life for all of us. Of course, we weren't the only ones; many other families from around the world sought the same ideals with their move to the land of the free and home of the brave. When my father finished his medical studies, we moved to California so my father could work for the Veterans Administration [VA] Hospital.

At first, nothing really made us stand out. We spoke English in our home. We had a big, sweet family dog and all the other trappings that helped us blend in with our neighbors. Life was pretty simple for me, and I considered myself a happy, typical American.

That was about to change dramatically.

On November 4, 1979, the United States embassy in Tehran, Iran, was taken hostage. The fifty-three hostages were held for 444 days until January 20, 1981.

Suddenly, as the daughter of Iranian-born parents, I stood out from my friends. Nothing would be *normal* again. I no longer felt like I was just like everyone else.

That's when I started getting bullied at school, and it only escalated from there. I was physically attacked on more than a few occasions. The thought of going to school terrified me. My brother started showing up at school to threaten the boys who were harassing me. It worked for a while. The physical taunting stopped, but the feeling of being an outcast lingered.

Then it happened. Instead of running from the taunts and attacks, I fought back. In fact, I fought everyone and everything that got in my way. When the unexpected comes at us—without trust in God—we learn to survive on our own strength. We do the only thing we can control, which means taking matters into our own hands.

That's exactly what I did.

At the tender age of thirteen, I started making *really* bad choices. A good example? A girlfriend and I took a bus to meet a total stranger at his house one day. Almost immediately after we knocked on his door, he took me up to his bedroom and forced me to perform oral sex on him.

I was *only* thirteen. I left his house feeling ashamed and confused. In fact, I was not entirely sure what had actually happened.

Unfortunately, he was friends with many boys at my school, and it didn't take long for word to get out about what had happened. Overnight, I became very popular with the boys. Even though I knew what they wanted and that it was wrong, I loved the attention. It was humiliating, but it was far better than being bullied and beaten up. As a result, I freely gave pieces of my soul away, and every time I did, I lost another part of myself.

That is where it all began—the social pressure to succeed at any cost. My self-esteem plummeted. The emotional abuse escalated with every relationship from then on. It definitely took a toll on who I became.

In many ways, I lived a charmed existence—certainly one that very few teenagers ever experience. By this time, my father was in private medical practice and doing well financially, so we lived in Beverly Hills. We went to dinner clubs every weekend, dancing and drinking the night away. We traveled to Las Vegas monthly, and I was even pulled out of school to catch a flight for one of those trips! It's no wonder that by the time I was fourteen, I was drinking nearly every weekend. It didn't take long for my drinking to become excessive.

By the time I was in high school, I smoked a pack of cigarettes a day and took prescription diet pills. Astonishingly, even with all of that, I did exceptionally well in school, was wickedly smart, and knew how to keep my destructive actions a secret.

When I wasn't partying with my family, I was at nightclubs with my friends. To this day I have no idea how I survived and didn't injure anyone else by driving drunk so frequently. During high school, I had a predictable routine: I went to school year-round, was a straight-A student, worked at my father's medical practice, went to nightclubs, and got wasted every weekend.

Alcohol, nightclubs, cigarettes, boys—and by then, I was also a bully. I went from the one who got picked on to the one who fought and picked on others. Once, I even got suspended for throwing a girl in a trash can.

My experience with racism at that early age left me really confused about my identity. I had no relationship with God because my parents did not practice Islam when we were growing up. I was born and raised as an American, yet I was identified as a foreigner with a strange religion. All these contradictions caused a rage to build up inside me. I took this rage out on myself and others.

Beverly Hills was and remains a cutthroat city. Everything was a competition during my adolescence. Nothing was enough, even though I was fortunate to have more than most—designer clothes, boyfriends, expensive cars, and regular family vacations. In my mind, I was never pretty or rich enough, nor adequate in anything else to satisfy the people around me, much less myself. I corrected that perceived deficit by being the wild and vicious one.

I fell in love with my high school sweetheart and mistakenly believed I would marry him one day. However, his parents adamantly rejected the idea of us ever being married since he was Jewish while my family and I were Muslim. They wanted him to marry a Jewish girl. Not only was I completely crushed, but my racial identity came back to haunt me once again. *Who was I? Where did I belong?*

It wasn't until I was in college that I fully understood how broken I was. My relationship with my parents was a constant paradox: I did everything they *asked* me to, yet I did everything I *wanted* to do in secret. When it came to my career, my heart's desire was to go into the military or law enforcement, but my father would not allow it. That's why I chose law, thinking that, at the very least, I could still fight on behalf of others.

Every relationship I chose until then was out of self-hatred and in defiance of my parents. Each toxic relationship broke me in very fundamental ways. At that point, I never fully learned how to feel or process my conflicted emotions.

Halfway through college, my father insisted I marry a Persian Muslim. Pleasing my father mattered a lot to me, and deep down, I knew he was probably right about marrying someone from my own culture. Yet, the stubborn streak in me wanted to do it my way. In my rebellion, I married the first good-looking Persian guy I could find who was as defiant and rebellious as I was. My parents disliked him, but my father permitted the marriage so I would settle down. Though we never talked about it directly, my father knew I was out of control. He thought the marriage would tame me. Well, that lasted all of six months. In the end, I was more damaged than before.

I started to feel something completely foreign. I was desperate for a relationship with God. Despite all the poor choices I had made, somewhere inside, I knew the only way to feel whole would be to find a relationship with Him. In my last year of undergraduate university, I met an Egyptian guy who introduced me to Islam. I was excited at the chance to finally fit in, but even that was short-lived. His community and their extremist interpretation of Islam alienated the American in me. I hated what that represented. I wanted no part of it. I was stuck in two worlds: one as the nice Persian Muslim and the other as the wild American girl.

Plenty of men continued to enter the picture, but none of them filled the hole in my soul. I knew in my heart that I needed God, and that desire led me to a spiritual Muslim group that felt real and made me feel a sense of belonging.

Around this time, my immediate family also became practicing Muslims. My father started asking his relatives about our family lineage, and he discovered the certified family tree that showed we were direct descendants of the prophet Muhammad. It seemed only natural that I would end up a devout Muslim.

I committed to being a practicing Muslim, kept an arduous prayer schedule, fulfilled the demanding fasting requirements, wore the headdress, and obeyed the strict daily clothing requirements. By this time, I had graduated from law school and had to decide on a future career. I served my Muslim community by helping with legal issues like contracts, hiring employees, and running a nonprofit that gave to charity and advocated for social issues. I also helped with real estate transactions and immigration cases. Despite how awkward and suffocating the rituals were, I did it all with the same fervor to succeed that I had dedicated to my other achievements.

I earned a traditional degree in Islamic jurisprudence under the tutelage of Sunni Muslim scholars, yet the more I learned, the more afraid I became of damnation. I was intensely aware of my colorful past and feared God would never forgive me for the things I had done. In Islam, no one can promise you forgiveness. You have NO way of knowing you will be accepted into paradise despite your devotion or because of your shortcomings. Your eternal security hangs in the balance, and it is impossible to determine the scale god would use. These fears lingered as the years went by, even though I succeeded professionally in ways that sometimes surprised even me. I tried to put my worries aside, move past and defeat them, but in the end, I could not.

2
TWO

Life in D.C.

When I was presented with an opportunity to fight Islamic extremism in Washington, D.C., I jumped at it. I packed my bags and left California, hoping never to return. Beverly Hills had crushed me, and I had the chance to start fresh. I stayed committed to my Muslim duties, and my career flourished.

Despite misgivings, I forged ahead and made tremendous professional strides. In a career spanning more than two decades, I held various positions, including president of a thriving nonprofit organization, a visiting scholar to Washington D.C.'s most prominent think tanks, and a political officer in the U.S. Embassy in Afghanistan.

It was not long before I realized that Washington, D.C., was just as cutthroat as Beverly Hills. If I wanted to succeed, I had to fight for all the contracts that would give me an advantage in my field. Fighting was something I knew well, and I beat out my competition time and time again. I often was more clever and manipulative than my colleagues. Everything in my life had become transactional; I would give of myself only if I would get something in return.

One of my most important professional accomplishments was creating the *first* evidence-based counter-radicalization program in the U.S. It was nationally recognized as a best practice in community policing and terrorism prevention. That success led to my appointment as senior advisor to FBI Headquarters, which fulfilled a childhood dream.

I was tasked with scaling and replicating the program I built in the private sector to prevent terrorism across our nation. I would travel around the country and assist local field offices and joint terrorism task forces with how to create similar programs in cities across the U.S. I would train them on the theories behind what radicalizes people to violence, as well as the community and law enforcement methods to thwart the process and build resilience against violence.

I enjoyed every minute of my new position. I loved the rush I got from serving my country in a way that felt impactful and important. About six months into the role, I decided it would feel more comfortable walking the halls of the Bureau without a headcover. I was annoyed by the awkward stares every time I walked into a room. I wanted to be known for my talents, not the fabric on my head. Nothing could have prepared me for the reaction that happened both from within the Muslim community and inside my own heart. Some Islamic scholars teach that if a woman takes off her head covering, she will hang by her hair for eternity in hell. I was shunned by community members who were shocked at my defiance.

After more than two decades of a life filled with painful contradictions, secrecy, and unfulfilled desires for peace, I slowly became convinced that something was *seriously* wrong in my life. I started to question everything—my religion, lifestyle choices, prayer life, and relationships. I mean *everything*. Something inside me just started to detach. It felt like the stronghold of Islam broke right off of me. That god was so cruel and unpredictable that I no longer could worship him. I resolved, then, to live a life without a relationship with god. What happened as a result was that my life, both personal and professional, was in utter chaos.

Meanwhile, at the FBI, my boss recommended me as a permanent hire, so I had to undergo a much more invasive exam: the Lifestyle Polygraph. Before entering the FBI, I underwent a very rigorous background check and passed a counter-intelligence polygraph. I was issued the highest-level top-secret security clearance to effectively execute the duties of my new position. However, for the lifestyle exam, the examiners ask about every facet of your personal life. Ironically, despite taking the polygraph several times, I couldn't pass a simple question about my personal life: Was I married? The reason that question was so troubling is because I was secretly the mistress of a married man. In Islam, I was referred to as a second wife, but I knew for a fact I was not married. Hence, I could not in good conscience answer that question either yes or no.

It soon became evident that my life, as I knew it, was coming to a crashing halt. My career would not continue as it was because I was not a credible Muslim. Looking back, I can laugh and say Jesus was going full "scorched earth" on me. I had to lose everything and come to Him empty-handed.

I thought Islam would make me feel safe, as though I was protected in a gilded cage. After all, I was a descendant of the founder of the faith. Nothing could have been further from the truth. It became apparent to me that the life of a devout Muslim woman is anything *but* safe. I had to accept that women were objects—nothing more than possessions to men. Any man who wanted could take a second or even a third wife. Any woman could be discarded just by a man uttering a few words, "I divorce you, I divorce you, I divorce you." Children born in this way have no legal protection, either. This was not a recent development in Muslim culture; it did not happen only in Saudi Arabia. I, like many thousands of other American women, was living this abusive lifestyle right here in the U.S. I was living out a generational curse that my ancestors had practiced for centuries.

Reflecting back on the experience reminds me of the Biblical story of Joseph. He was left for dead in a ditch by his brothers and then sold into slavery to the Egyptians. Even with that blistering beginning, he had access to people and experiences he otherwise never would have had. His challenging experience was part of his journey to victory. As I thought about Joseph's experience and compared it to mine, I understood there was purpose in every step I took. While I was going through it, I was a slave to the unworthy men in my life and to the religious law that kept me in bondage. At the time, I could not see a way out and resolved to accept my situation. I even convinced myself I was lucky it wasn't worse.

T H R E E

The Extraction

God literally extracted me from the Islamic faith. Suddenly, I had the opportunity to escape, and I took it. The strangest twist in leaving Islam was that nothing in me had changed. As the old saying goes, "When you go, you take you with you." I ended up getting into another broken relationship, yet this time, the wreckage would be far greater.

Instead of making better choices, I fell right into the arms of another married man. He was extremely demanding, critical, and unfaithful. He was not a Muslim, but he also didn't care if I was. It was ridiculous that I would fall into that same trap, but again, it was transactional. We went into business together and made a fortune doing so. I let the financial incentives outweigh the horrible moral and social implications of what I was doing. I had no moral compass.

As a devout Muslim, I did not engage in any of the debauchery of my youth. I was sober almost twenty-five years, and yet all my vices quickly returned with a vengeance. That's not all—my aggressive streak was at an all-time high. I got into physical altercations with my boyfriend, broke kitchen glasses, and screamed obscenities. Looking back, I can't believe how ugly it was!

After I permanently removed my head covering and finally left Islam officially, I was excommunicated. I lost everything and everyone from that world. I moved back home to Beverly Hills—a place I hated—but I desperately needed the love and support of my parents.

The battles I had with my boyfriend escalated to a boiling point, and we both knew the relationship was very toxic. We could not amicably end our business ties, so we ended up in a nasty lawsuit with no end in sight. We both wanted utter destruction for one another. By this point, I was emotionally and intellectually shattered. All my clever maneuvering and manipulative practices couldn't get me out of the hole I had dug for myself.

In my despair, I came across a tweet from a stranger who posted a clip from her celebrity pastor. She said his sermons had healed her of her emotional trauma. This piqued my curiosity. Wanting to know how a pastor could be so inspirational, I watched the video.

The pastor's message was simple, "Give your life to Jesus, and He will make you whole again." Her Jesus had the power to save you from Hell and promised eternal salvation. I had never heard of *that* Jesus! The Jesus I knew in Islam was just a prophet. None of my Christian colleagues in D.C. ever preached the simple Gospel to me. I had no idea Jesus promised eternal security and could restore me to wholeness. It was like listening to a Christian Tony Robbins seminar. I was filled with hope and motivation. Most of all, I was filled with the desire to learn more about the Jesus of the Bible. To put it plainly, I was hooked.

After binge-watching this pastor on YouTube for more than a month, I started praying for God to reveal Himself. While that sounds simple and straightforward, I was wracked with confusion when I considered that Jesus was God. Muslims are taught that believing in the Trinity violates God's oneness. However, I was far too invested and needed to finish what I had started.

The Gospel message impacted me in ways I couldn't even understand at that time. It was as if God knew exactly what I needed to hear at this point in my life. I heard Him speak to me through this pastor, telling me how to solve my problems right in the middle of this very messy business and personal breakup! I thought God was drawing me to the message of Christ so that I could resolve a dispute with a Christian. I soon realized that He was calling *me* directly.

There I was, pleading with God to save me. I was on my knees, with my head on the floor in the traditional position of Muslim prayer known as *Sajda*, crying to God to lead me. Suddenly, I heard the voice of Christ. He called my name in the sweetest tone I have ever heard, "Hedieh, it's Me."

The experience of pleading with God to reveal Himself to me and then hearing His voice was a supernatural encounter that was impossible to deny or ignore. I started crying hysterically, then sat up and was shocked. After that sublime experience, I had an overwhelming fear of what it would mean to become a Christian. For Muslims to accept Christ meant they were marked for death. Officials in any Muslim country to which I traveled could arrest me and charge me with apostasy. That's not the worst of it, either. Any crazed Muslim in the United States could take it upon himself to impose the ultimate penalty—death. My family would surely disown me.

That's not exactly a happily ever after.

I bought my first Bible and spent the next few years devouring Scripture and studying Biblical commentary regarding the messages I was absorbing. I was living alone with my daughter and rarely left the house because I had to reconcile my heart and intellect to the fact that Jesus was God incarnate. I prayed incessantly as I read and marveled at how the Scriptures came to life. The Lord revealed to me what steps He took to draw man to Him. I was reading the love story of God to each and every one of us. Salvation ultimately culminated in the sacrifice of His only begotten Son so we can be in right standing with Him.

Learning about the Gospel of Christ made me feel entirely transformed from within. I couldn't and wouldn't let go. The more I learned, the more in love with Him I became. The Bible literally spoke to me. It answered all my questions about how Christ fit into my understanding of God and religion.

Still, I worried about my family and how to share that I believed Christ is God. The only person I could trust to tell was my therapist. I told her Jesus showed up when I prayed to God. She was quite shocked, too.

"Jesus?"

"Yeah, Jesus," I replied.

She tried to walk me through the range of emotions I was feeling. Since she was a Catholic, she was very helpful in the process. She suggested a compromise. I could get help and love from Jesus *without* becoming a Christian. I couldn't accept that because I knew that Jesus was drawing me to Him powerfully and beautifully. I hadn't felt that good in a very long time. I didn't want it to stop.

Nearly every day, I would listen to the pastor on my car radio, driving my daughter to and from school. He said, "Invite Jesus into every aspect of your life—into every situation. Your car can even be your prayer closet." My car was *already* my prayer closet because it was often the only place I was alone. I prayed that prayer, and sure enough, I felt the image of Christ sitting right next to me in the car! He put His hand on my hand and said, "My daughter, you don't have to be afraid anymore." I began crying so hysterically that I had to pull over. No truer words have ever been spoken to me.

I later learned the Lord said similar words to John:

> *"When I saw Him, I fell at His feet as though dead. Then He placed His right hand on me and said: 'Do not be afraid. I am the First and the Last.'"*

> *—Revelation 1:17*

FOUR

Becoming New in Christ

I traveled to North Carolina to be baptized at the megachurch of the pastor to whom I was originally drawn. A group of extraordinary believers surrounded me. One lady I had only met on the phone offered to fly and meet me so I would not be alone. Three of her friends, whom I did not even know, drove twelve hours from Virginia to join us. Their kindness and unconditional love was something I had never experienced. Why would four complete strangers go through all that trouble for me? I was overwhelmed with gratitude and joy. They supported me through the emotional upheaval of telling family and friends I was now a Christ follower. One of the ladies remained a mentor to me for years. She instructed me on the importance of prayer and reading Scripture. She helped me understand how to listen for God's voice and live a life that reflects God's holiness.

She encouraged me to draw closer to God's Word and live the life the disciples described for a believer through the Gospel. I could not have matured as a follower of Christ without her discipleship.

"For we are His workmanship, created in Christ Jesus for good works, which God prepared beforehand that we should walk in them."

—*Ephesians 2:10*

So, exactly what is a Christ follower? Christ followers have steadfast faith in the One sent to save us from ourselves. They do their best to obey Him and go throughout their lives enjoying a relationship with the Living God.

I have since dedicated my life to accomplishing the purpose He has given me to advance the Kingdom of God, no matter the consequences it may have for me. I have been a warrior, trying to overcome evil for a long time. Suffering and sacrifice are not foreign to me. I have always known in my spirit:

"If God is for us, who can be against us?"

—*Romans 8:31*

Now, the difference is I actually know who God IS. Some people who hear about my conversion assume there's inconsistency in my faith. Frankly, the opposite is true. My understanding of the reality of Jesus as God is what He destined for me from the very beginning. He took me the long route through the wilderness so I could reach back and help others. My journey can help other Muslims experience the freedom from sin and bondage that comes only through faith in Christ as our Lord and Savior. As the Apostle Paul emphatically proclaims:

"This righteousness is given through faith in Jesus Christ to all who believe. There is no difference between Jew and Gentile, for all have sinned and fall short of the glory of God, and all are justified freely by His grace through the redemption that came by Christ Jesus."

—*Romans 3:21–24*

All these experiences were possible since any of us can meet Jesus—anywhere. The power of the internet to spread the Gospel and make it accessible to every corner of the earth is really quite extraordinary.

I pray that people will meet Jesus in a way they never could have imagined. If you haven't met Him, please know He will meet you wherever you are. He will reach out His hand and pull you out of whatever cave or ditch you are in. He will fill all your empty places with His unconditional love. He will never leave. He will never let you down. He will show you the most beautiful and perfect version of you—even as He gently walks you through the ugly parts you need to fix. It's an unselfish, unconditional, loving walk with your Heavenly Father, who wants only the absolute best for you.

> *"For I know the plans I have for you," declares the Lord. "Plans to prosper you and not to harm you, plans to give you hope and a future."*
>
> —*Jeremiah 29:11*

After my conversion, I reconnected with a dear friend and colleague who heard that I had accepted Christ. As we talked, she expressed her happiness for me, but she was disappointed I was no longer *fighting the good fight*. When I thought and prayed about what she said, I decided the truth was quite the opposite! I *am* still in the fight, but now I have a REAL solution. The power of Christ Jesus can save, transform, and redeem all humanity, even lost Muslims.

In my new battleground, my duty in this fight is to spread the good news of the Gospel and offer Muslims—and all of us, really— the *only* solution to a life filled with anger, vengefulness, and hatred. That solution is to accept the grace that abounds through a simple yet powerful profession of faith in Jesus as your Lord and Savior. As you do, watch your life go from darkness to light, bondage to freedom, and hatred to love.

5

— FIVE —

Breaking Chains

"At that moment the curtain of the temple was torn in two from top to bottom. The earth shook, the rocks split and the tombs broke open. The bodies of many holy people who had died were raised to life."

—Matthew 27:53

This expressive verse in Matthew describes what happened when Jesus Christ was crucified and then resurrected. The veil of the temple being torn and the rocks being split are what happens in our own bodies when we receive the blood of Christ and experience His resurrection. Suddenly, the veil between Heaven and earth is torn open, and the reality of Christ is revealed in our hearts and souls.

I love this analogy because it is exactly what I felt when I first met Jesus.

When I first encountered Christ, I was in the worst situation of my life—and believe me, I was used to getting myself out of difficult situations. I entered one bad relationship after another due in part to the social pressure to succeed at any cost. In the process, I suffered tremendous emotional abuse and was emotionally detached from the reality of my situation.

I didn't know until I went into therapy for the first time when I was fifty that I might have been suffering from *dissociative disorder*. That's just a fancy term for the ability to disassociate myself from all the painful consequences of my bad choices. It made it possible to live and often thrive in everyday circumstances that otherwise would have been intolerable. I lived only to survive. I had never learned how to live a healthy life by trusting my instincts.

At this point, no one could deny I was a victim. Even though I had a successful career and made a global impact in fighting Islamic extremism, I was morally bankrupt—completely and utterly broken.

The Webster's dictionary describes a victim as "one that is injured, destroyed, or sacrificed under any of various conditions" or "one that is subjected to oppression, hardship, or mistreatment."

A victim is oppressed when they are forcefully obligated to please some *one* or some *thing* at the expense of their own wellbeing and security. No matter how much one despises it or rebels momentarily, eventually, one can learn to forsake their welfare to gain acceptance and love. Doing so, in my case, led to angry outbursts, being short-tempered, abusing food, and engaging in other self-destructive behavior to compensate for not being free.

It is easy for someone on the outside to say, "Why didn't you just leave?" Well, if you have ever been subjected to emotional oppression and manipulation, you know it's never easy to just walk away. There can be grave social and financial consequences for doing so as well.

Before you know it, you are in a prison—a bondage with no obvious means of escape.

Like me, you could even end up in bondage to *god*—or at least that's what you're told. This bondage forces you to sacrifice everything because your eternal life is at stake. The religion convinces you that you must obey his laws if you really want him to love you and forgive your sins. Yet, when you peel back that *religion*, you learn that what some claim to be god's laws are actually a distortion of ancient religious scripture, combined with a set of cultural norms from faraway lands that are completely alien to us living in the twenty-first century.

You do *not* have to live that way forever.

It took almost twenty-five years for me to figure out that I was in bondage. Even though the strict rules forced onto Muslim women never felt comfortable for me, it wasn't easy to walk away. Muslim women are repeatedly taught that the shackles placed on their minds and bodies are a blessing and a form of protection. I bought into that for many years until this quiet voice in my heart convinced me to walk away.

Take a moment to evaluate your own relationships. Do you see a pattern of going from one abusive or manipulative relationship to another? Are you a helpless victim in bondage to a parent, sibling, spouse, or other loved one? Is there a voice deep inside of you begging to be free, but you have accepted this cycle as your lot in life?

In the Bible, the Apostles recount the meeting between Jesus and the Samaritan woman of ill repute. Jesus starts a conversation with this woman at Jacob's well by asking her for a drink of water. It was surprising He would even talk to a woman like her. She wasn't Jewish and was obviously of a lower status. She was at the well alone, and during the hot afternoon—women of higher status went to the well at dawn.

Jesus tells her about her life and how she's looking for love in all the wrong places. He then promises her the water of *life*, which would forever quench her thirst for acceptance and love. She immediately realized He must be the Messiah because He knew her deepest secrets and needs.

She knew nothing about Him, what He preached, the miracles He performed, or even the Old Testament, yet she became one of the first evangelists for Christ. Her faith and passion for the message of freedom made her whole village run after Christ.

I love her story since her message of Jesus is simple. Come meet the Messiah, have faith in Him, and He will set you free. All she needed was that *truth* to make people believe.

I see similarities of my journey in this passage. I am not a Bible scholar. I was not a believer in Christ my whole life. Not even a single one of my family members was Christian. However, I encountered the Son of the One living God, which changed my life forever.

I believe that many of my past experiences were divinely engineered for such a time as this. That reality can be the same for you if you let Him in. You, too, can be born again in Christ. He is the One who gave His life for all of us, to be free—a priceless gift we didn't earn and surely didn't deserve.

A victim is someone too broken or too weak to articulate or defend their own needs. When someone gives their life to Jesus Christ, they no longer are a victim.

In Romans 8, we learn that we are no longer in bondage to a set of laws, regardless of their religious origin. We cannot be a slave to another human being. Each and every one of us can have a personal, internal relationship with the Triune God, who always wants the best for us and works everything for our good. He is never selfish, greedy, or corrupt. He never fails to show up, and He is the ultimate guide to the best version of you.

In Romans 8, we also learn that we are free to discover and experience what it means to be loved unconditionally and free from the threats of sin and damnation. Jesus bore the penalty of all our sins and guaranteed our salvation simply through faith. He affirms for us that we are perfect exactly as He created us, complete with all our gifts and flaws. He points us toward our true purpose that will give our life meaning and fulfillment.

You will be victorious!

These are not just words or slogans to make us feel good. When we truly live by these principles, we begin to see life and relationships in a whole new way. I realized that as a victim, my character flaws of anger, resentment, and unforgiveness were the result of feeling caged and helpless to overcome the injustices and escape my predicament. Once the grace that comes through faith started to permeate my life, I could forgive the wrongs that were done to me and move forward. I no longer allowed the pain to shackle me to the past. I was filled with hope for the future I had in Christ.

SIX

Overcoming Destructive Patterns

"The Lord is righteous. He has cut me free from the cords of the wicked."

—Psalm 129:4

Though I knew accepting Christ made me a new creation and His righteousness was within me, I had to resolve the patterns in my heart and mind that kept drawing me back into destructive behavior. I would describe that process, which is still ongoing, in four essential steps.

The first step is *surrender.* Once we repent from sin and accept Christ as our Lord and Savior, we are immediately granted salvation and freedom from the penalty of sin. Our sins are nailed to the cross and are left there. We can let go of shame and regret. We can eliminate grudges as we exercise and experience the power of forgiveness. Our *whole being will be changed.* However, surrender also means giving up control, not to another human being but to God.

The second step is to *listen for the voice of God through the indwelling of the Holy Spirit.* This is a deeply personal, one-on-one journey. The notion that God would talk directly to me was difficult to imagine. I used to ask my mentor whether I was waiting for a conversation with a burning bush. How would I know I was hearing the voice of God and not my own desires or even the devil?

She repeatedly and gently reminded me, "You just have to talk to Him, pray, and read the Bible. You'll know when you hear Him."

She was right. I knew the moment I heard God speak to me. You will, too.

The third step is *self-awareness and alignment with the Holy Spirit.* That means we do everything in our power to partner with the Holy Spirit to ensure that our actions, character, and behavior are more like Christ. We are not on autopilot like a Tesla! We have to be willing to yield our passions and desires to God. In that surrender, He will align our thoughts and actions to His will. He will cast out anything evil.

"We are taking every thought captive to the obedience of Christ."

—*2 Corinthians 10: 5*

Our goal is to live in accordance with God's purpose for our life. Change your perspective so you can forgive others as well as yourself. Remember, Jesus came to seek and save the lost. That's all of us!

Once you have completed the other steps, the fourth and final step is to use what you have learned to *live out your God-given potential.* Always remember that your calling is specific to you! Don't look to others as you work to figure out your calling. God gave them a certain calling, and He gave one to you that is exclusively yours. He will give you the grace to run your race because you are uniquely suited to accomplish this purpose.

The interesting part of living out your purpose is that *it's already written.* Your victory has already been won. You'll likely realize that only in the end stages of life as you look back on what has transpired. God's timing is an important part of that, so continue to go forward in faith and seek what He may be trying to tell you.

SEVEN

Getting Ready for Battle

"Do not be afraid of those who kill the body but cannot kill the soul. Rather, be afraid of the One who can destroy both soul and body in hell."

—Matthew 10:28

When I first became a Christian, I looked forward to a quiet life, basking in the love and beauty of meeting my Lord and Savior. Such a thing was very appealing to me. I had spent most of my adult life deeply engrossed in political battles over one issue or another, as well as serving my country in ways that were quite dangerous.

After all of that, I was pleased at the prospect of calm and tranquility.

Not even six months passed before I realized that the peaceful life I had anticipated as a Christian was not going to be the norm. I clearly understood that I was going back into battle.

Within those few months, the Lord gave me the vision for my ministry so that I would help others experience the redemptive power of Christ. At first, I wanted to ignore the call and pretend I didn't hear it correctly. Why? Starting a ministry and being public with my Christian faith meant I could be attacked or even physically harmed by Muslims who wanted to impose the penalty of apostasy. As I mentioned earlier, that penalty includes death. *Battle* was almost an understatement.

Ignoring the call wasn't an option. The Lord was relentless. The inspirations came to me like a flood nearly every day. Finally, I heard His words, "Hedieh, you are battle-tested, combat-ready." Those words made me laugh out loud because they were so true. My whole life and career prepared me for this new mission—to spread the Gospel when being a follower of Christ is increasingly under attack.

I have lived and worked in numerous places where my life and safety were often at risk. I barely escaped the bombing of Beirut during the war in 2006 and survived being shot at in downtown Damascus. I nearly lost my toes from frostbite under house arrest by a Central Asian dictator whose staff forgot to turn on the heat when it was twenty degrees below zero. I even survived the Tsunami in Southeast Asia and confrontation with more than a few suspected terrorists. The Lord combined all the inner fortitude and discipline of my past with the courage and strength that comes from being in a relationship with Him. He intended to use it all so I could serve the Kingdom.

It is no wonder being thrust into direct conflict over my political opinions or the vicious responses to my Christian Post articles did not scare or deter me.

"Blessed are you when others revile you and persecute you and utter all kinds of evil against you falsely on my account. Rejoice and be glad, for your reward is great in Heaven."

—*Matthew 5:11-12*

My faith in Christ is at the forefront of all I do, whether I am writing columns, producing a podcast, doing radio interviews, witnessing to my hairstylist, or speaking out at a school board meeting. I will be honest, though, it is the cause of great conflict.

I know that my life transition would be too daunting for most people. Losing access to loved ones, being taunted by total strangers for what you believe, or having your children subjected to ridicule because of your choices is *hard*. Even seasoned Christians are frightened about subjecting themselves to "battle." It is not surprising that those who hear me boldly share my spiritual journey are often alarmed to see how outspoken I am.

Christ knew the extraordinary experiences of my career prepared me for the greatest and most important challenge of my life—becoming a warrior for Christ.

While those extreme encounters tested my strength, the Holy Spirit's power within me gave me the courage I now possess within every cell of my body. I have always considered myself to be strong, but this is supernatural fortitude I had *never* experienced before salvation.

The most important message here is that I'm not the only one who can be bold and outspoken for God's truth. It is available to *all* who accept Jesus Christ as their Lord and Savior.

I've learned many crucial lessons since becoming a Christian that even all my previous experiences didn't teach me. Alongside strength and courage, I have learned that a warrior for Christ must have the fruit of the Spirit—namely kindness, gentleness, forbearance, and self-control. Sometimes, the Lord signals us to stay quiet and let the storm pass. This concept was entirely new to me. Before my salvation, I was the first to retaliate for an offense, real or perceived. Now, I wait for prompting from the Holy Spirit to guide me as to when and how to respond.

In all my years, when I was practicing Islam, I never learned or even considered most of these attributes, least of all kindness or gentleness. I worked in the very fast-paced, competitive industry of federal contracting, so I was always fighting my way to the top. To be successful, I had to work hard and be ruthless against the competition. I did both of those things. Good character was not part of the equation. Back then, if I prayed, fasted, and wore a headcover, I figured I was good with "god." Life was just a series of transactions, even love. I always tried to give something in exchange for receiving what I wanted.

It was not until I encountered the Gospel that I learned about unconditional love. I began to understand the significance of gentleness, kindness, and forbearance in the face of adversity. Jesus was loving, kind, and forgiving, no matter what was done to Him. He gave it all for us to be free. My love affair with Jesus made me want to be more like Him. I realized how far I still had to go.

In living through what seems to be a prolonged season of social and political unrest, the ability to hold my tongue has been incredibly valuable. So many people, including me, are reacting to world events based on their personal trauma. The Lord has taught me not to react emotionally. He continues to show me the reality of my situation through prayer and His Word. He shows me how to respond with wisdom and guidance through the Holy Spirit. One of the most beautiful expressions I heard the Lord whisper to me was, "Hedieh, spend more time reading the Word. Walk with me. Learn my ways."

EIGHT

The Battlegrounds

"Do not suppose that I have come to bring peace on earth. I did not come to bring peace, but a sword."

—Matthew 10:34

How do we know when it's time to stand our ground? We will understand through spiritual discernment. Jesus warned us that we would face battles and hardships to prepare us, not *scare* us. Many Bible verses teach us *how* to protect ourselves when the enemy attacks. For example:

"The weapons of our warfare are not carnal, but mighty through God for the pulling down of strongholds"

—2 Corinthians 10:4.

We learn to draw on the spirit realm for strength and defense in the struggle against evil forces. Christ also made it clear that physical trials may come to us as well, beginning with the gruesome fates of His disciples to the current persecution of Christians throughout China, Iran, and the Middle East. Christians in America have been in the majority for centuries, and I worry that such a position of relative comfort has not helped them prepare for persecution and hardship. Those of us from the Middle East and Africa have lived through bloody civil wars and lawlessness. Surviving persecution is a way of life for us. It is fascinating that the Lord, in His infinite wisdom, is calling so many of us into salvation for such a time as this. I firmly believe that those who have survived consistent persecution will use those experiences to help strengthen their Christian brethren.

Throughout my career, I listened to many potential terrorists who had one thing in common: how they described Christians. Most of them said that Christians are "weak in spirit and discipline" or "Christians don't know what it means to die for their god." As a believer, I now see how those words should *never* be used to describe a follower of Christ!

The courage of a follower of Christ comes from knowing that we have the power of the Holy Spirit on our side. Christ lives within us to enable us to overcome any kind of obstacle. Every man dies, but very few *really* live. We have that choice because Jesus Christ died so that we can have life and life more abundantly. We must choose to stand in the power of the Lord, as described in Paul's epistle to the Ephesians:

> *"Finally, my brethren, be strong in the Lord and in the power of His might. Put on the whole armor of God, that you may be able to stand against the wiles of the devil"*
>
> *—Ephesians 6:10–11.*

That is how, as followers of Christ we stand our ground. We stand our ground, clothed and protected in the whole armor of God.

Part of that is preaching the Gospel with authority and power to deliver the good news of salvation through Christ. We should not be concerned with popularity, polls, or politics. We must deliver God's Word loudly to all His people. The great commission the Lord gave is a commandment for the believers to go and make disciples of all nations, teaching them to obey everything He commanded. No caveat says that we only do this when it is comfortable or that it is merely a suggestion among many options. It is commanded of us as followers.

God's truth is binary—it's not a spectrum. There's good and evil, truth and falsehood. Saying that is not being judgmental; it's being honest. I lived under the oppression of a false religion for decades. I refuse to lie about that to spare someone's feelings. I want all to experience the love and freedom that comes from accepting Christ.

All of us have problems. Jesus is the solution.

Whatever insults, ridicule, or intimidation is thrown at Christ followers, we cannot waiver nor change the truth of the Gospel. Only faith in Christ saves, heals, and redeems. In this time of turmoil, the world needs Jesus more than ever.

The next time you as a Christian are frightened by news reports, question whether you should defend your freedom to gather for worship, or defend the Gospel, remember the words of Jesus:

> *"Whatever I tell you in the dark, speak in the light; and what you hear in the ear, preach on the housetops."*
>
> *—Matthew 10:27*

PART 2

MY NEW FAMILY

"If anyone does not know how to manage his own family, how can he take care of God's church?"

—1 Timothy 3:5

NINE

Starting From Scratch

Looking back, I know without any doubt that God's hand was over my life the whole time. He took me first through the bondage of a life of sin. Then He took me to the "law of Islam." Then, He took me back to a life of sin and despair so that I could truly experience the freedom and salvation that comes through Christ.

I knew I had to leave Islam, but the situation I had gotten myself into was horrible! I had no idea where God was taking me. In fact, I wasn't sure at all that God was the one leading me. In all honesty, I felt like I was blindfolded and being dragged down a long tunnel.

I was so confused, and my thoughts demonstrated that confusion. *Why am I in this place? How did I get HERE? Don't You love me anymore? Wasn't I a faithful servant? Why am I in such a wretched state?*

God wanted to bring me to my knees, which wasn't easy, even for Him. He wanted me to have no way out but Him, no matter how unbelievable that way out seemed. He knew there was no other way I would have accepted that Christ was Lord!

Knowing God's hand has been over me the whole time brings me peace and allows me to forgive those who hurt me. All of it got me to where I am today. God wanted me to see His power, and He wanted to grant me salvation. I feel such deep gratitude and joy for my salvation that I can now thank those who pushed me away.

Walking with the Lord meant accepting that His transformational power would sometimes *hurt*. Undoing decades of false teaching, lack of moral character, debauchery—you name it—feels punishing. Funny enough, the Bible tells us we will have days like that.

> *"We've been surrounded and battered by troubles, but we're not demoralized; we're not sure what to do, but we know God knows what to do. We've been spiritually terrorized, but God hasn't left our side; we've been thrown down, but we haven't broken."*
>
> —*2 Corinthians 4:8 MSG*

Why? So that we can put to death our old selves and be remade in the image of Christ. For the first several years of my new journey, I barely left the house. I felt too disoriented and wanted the transformation to take root. I took my daughter to school, visited with my parents, and did essential shopping. I also found a local church nearby that welcomed my daughter and me. I was excited to be a part of a community of believers.

The ladies were very kind and included me in their evening Bible study. I enjoyed their company and was grateful for their warm embrace of us. I continued my personal studies of the Bible through Logos software and the plethora of commentaries it made available to better understand Scripture. Online, I was also still very much a part of the megachurch where I was baptized and first came to saving faith.

The megachurch pastor rarely spoke of repentance. He did not emphasize the importance of turning away from sin. He did not warn about false teachers and the level of deception that would occur before Christ's return. He almost entirely ignored the book of Revelation. Each of his sermons covered only one or two verses of the Bible, often the same ones repeatedly.

My first pastor was definitely charismatic and led me to explore what Christ had to offer. Yet, as I matured in the Gospel, I needed more. My mentor referred me to other pastors online to develop a deeper understanding of Scripture. She wanted me to grow in the Word. The most prominent was Pastor Jack Hibbs of Calvary Chapel Chino Hills [CCCH].

Had the Lord not led me to seek out the true teachings of the Bible, I would have stayed in the megachurch—after all, it was the "cool place to be." It was not until I listened to Pastor Jack Hibbs that I realized how little I had learned about the Bible from that megachurch. It left me without the solid foundation I needed to withstand the storms of life.

I was really excited to learn that Pastor Jack Hibbs and CCCH were within driving distance from my home, so I planned to visit in person. I had a close friend of mine, Jim, who attended the church and knew my conversion story. He thought Pastor Jack would be encouraged by my testimony, and he took a chance to see if we could arrange a personal introduction. We were pleasantly surprised to hear that Pastor Jack was willing to meet with us. I was so excited!

Meanwhile, I was launching my ministry online with the help of Salem Media. When I went to their offices for a brainstorming session, the general manager heard of my upcoming visit to Pastor Jack and called me into his office. His advice was clear and direct: "Be sure you ask Jack to be your spiritual covering; you're going to need it." I was taken aback by it; honestly, I did not know what it meant. Nonetheless, the instruction stuck in my mind.

A few weeks later, my dear friend Jim and I, along with his friend Carlos, who had been a member of CCCH for decades, went to meet with Pastor Jack. He was gracious in listening to my story and gave us much of his valuable time. In the end, I asked that fateful question: "Terry told me to ask if you would be my spiritual covering."

Without a pause, Pastor Jack responded, "Yes, of course. If anyone questions your faith, and believe me, some will—send them to me." I started weeping uncontrollably. All three men were speechless at my reaction. Then Pastor Jack said, "Why are you crying?" To which I responded, "I cannot believe you would do that for me. I am a total stranger, and you have agreed to help me unconditionally." It was a pivotal moment and would change the trajectory of my life forever.

From that day on, I committed to going to CCCH and driving to Chino every week from Brentwood. I wanted to learn as much as possible and knew that was where I would grow and mature in my faith.

On the very first Sunday at CCCH, I sat alone in the first row. I was a bit nervous not knowing anyone, but then a woman came directly next to me and sat down with her husband. She turned to me and said something along the lines of, "You are new here. My name is Jolene, and the Lord told me to sit with you. Tell me your story." It felt like I was talking with a long-lost family member, and we were catching up on the past 50 years. Jolene is a seasoned saint who discipled women on Biblical marriage. Over the next couple of years, sitting next to each other every Sunday and talking on the phone, I learned what it meant to be a Biblically-based woman and wife.

At this point in my walk, I was still very focused on what the Lord was pruning out of me, and it was not pretty. I would pray and cry uncontrollably, repenting and asking Jesus for healing. I visited several churches that had deliverance ministries, and each time one of the saints prayed over me, I felt strongholds breaking. In those quiet times with the Lord, we talked about His promise to me that I would have a traditional marriage. I dreamed of that my whole life. Yet, all the men I knew convinced me it was impossible. "You are too strong," they would say. "No man could take your independence and defiant attitude." I had not realized that curse over me had a large part to do with why I would accept being a concubine, a mistress to a man over 25 years older than me. I thought I did not deserve better. Well, the Lord spoke over me about how that curse was broken. In Christ, I would experience a faithful marriage covenant—one man and one woman until death do us part.

I became like a lost Cinderella, wandering around looking for my Prince Charming. In the process, I met a whole bunch of frogs! I started to write in my journal about the qualities in a man that appealed to me and heard what the Lord was calling me to expect. No more manipulation, debauchery, or adultery. I needed a husband who was filled with the Spirit and loved Jesus as much as I did. Jolene kept encouraging me to look for men in our church. She said the Lord directed me to that church for sound doctrine and community. Building a community meant having a family also rooted in the same church. Honestly, I did not believe meeting someone there would be likely, but she was confident I would.

Meanwhile, my daughter and I moved to Ventura County, 65 miles away from Chino. She was going to attend a prestigious private Christian school. I was commuting almost two hours each way to church on Sunday. Some days, at 4 am, I could feel the Holy Spirit literally pushing me out of bed to go to church. I considered finding a church locally, but the Holy Spirit convicted me that I could not move.

TEN

The Fairytale Meeting

When COVID-19 first struck the nation, the churches were closed indefinitely. However, Pastor Jack reopened after six weeks. We were one of only a handful of churches that opened back up. We saw hundreds of new attendees each week. The church was bursting at the seams. One Saturday afternoon, the church hosted a "Non-Essentials Conference" to argue why churches are essential and to encourage other churches to open back up. I was standing in a very long line outside, and after about 20 minutes, I turned around to find a man standing behind me with a big smile on his face. You may laugh at this, but he was glowing! We were instantly drawn to each other and spent the rest of the day talking and laughing. He took my phone number and called me that night.

We talked for hours about our careers, children, and walking with Jesus. We were both at church the following day, but he sat a couple of rows behind me. In the middle of worship, the Lord was speaking to my heart. He recited to me *every* quality I was looking for in a spouse, written in my journal. He had placed all those qualities in this man I met. Only the Lord knew that list. The Lord wanted me to know for certain this is the man who I was destined to marry. I began weeping out of joy and fear. The next words I heard were, "And don't let him go." Yikes. What did that mean? I would soon learn.

Andy and I were inseparable from the day we met. The pandemic was still in effect, so all businesses were closed except fast food and Walmart. Our first date was in the parking lot at McDonald's with four out of five of Andy's kids. Wow, that was a lot of children. I was barely learning how to raise my own daughter.

ELEVEN

My Beautiful Little Girl

While living in D.C., I worked so hard and traveled so much that my daughter barely saw me. I had full-time nannies who looked out for her, but they were like a revolving door. By the time she was ten years old, we had gone through over a dozen caretakers. I really did not have maternal instincts. Supposedly, every mother has them upon the child's birth, but it felt like it skipped right over me. I treated motherhood as a responsibility to keep her safe and fed. Regrettably, I did not show the affection and love she really needed and craved.

Once I came to faith in Christ, my heart softened, and I felt an outpouring of compassion for my daughter beyond anything I had ever felt. I was grieved by how badly I had neglected her. Forgiving myself for that took a very long time, and gaining her forgiveness took even longer. I vowed to make it up to her, and she became the center of my existence. Did I overcompensate? You bet I did.

I told her about Andy and the kids. She had always dreamed of having a traditional family, so she was excited at the prospect of us dating. Unfortunately, the prestigious Christian school was also shut down, and my daughter was stuck at home with me. None of her friends could go out, and she buried herself in social media. I was clueless about how destructive it was becoming. At the same time, she was still reeling from losing all her blood relatives, both from my family and her father. She went from being surrounded by dozens of loving siblings, cousins, nieces, and friends to absolutely no one but her grandparents and me. She became distant and depressed. Her mental state continued to decline.

Often, the battle to uphold Biblical truths can be the most difficult when fought at home. My daughter was suffering from clinical depression, and during the COVID lockdowns, she was also struck with rapid-onset gender dysphoria. Though she attended a prestigious Christian school, the social isolation, her trauma from so much loss, indoctrination by social media, and a poor choice of friends convinced her that she was born the "wrong gender."

I sought out the best therapy for her that I could find. During a very quarrelsome meeting to discuss her sudden condition, the therapist wanted me to accept "her truth." I refused. I explained to both my daughter and the therapist that I knew God wanted a better life for her and that living a life of sin would never bring healing and restoration. My daughter cried throughout the whole meeting, but she knew she could never change my mind.

I gently and repeatedly explained that being a woman did not mean she could not have what society says are "male" qualities. She was God's daughter—strong, outspoken, resilient, and beautiful—just as He intended. In fact, she was just like me. I affirmed my unconditional love for her and my duty as a parent to proclaim these eternal principles, regardless of whether society said they were outdated or backward.

We had many painful nights filled with tears and feelings of hopelessness for both of us. Slowly, I saw her childhood joy return. She no longer claims to be the "wrong gender" and steadily appreciates how God made her. I share this heart-wrenching struggle because I experienced the blessings of standing on God's Word. Just as I would never give up on my daughter, we cannot give up on all our children, families, and this country. My daughter is just one of the thousands of kids being torn apart by the demonic forces at work in their lives.

TWELV

My Prince Charming

My relationship with Andy continued to flourish. We saw each other regularly, and then I caught COVID. It was miserable, but I recovered in a couple of days. Soon after, Andy was sick and kept getting worse. His breathing dangerously declined, and he went back and forth to the ER before finally being admitted. The doctors could not stabilize him. His kids had only met me once, and we lived 60 miles away from each other. His eldest daughter came to stay with the younger children while he was hospitalized. The doctor called me one night and asked for permission to take whatever means necessary to "save his life." I adamantly refused to permit them to intubate. I had barely known this man for a month and was already making life-saving decisions for him. I had to do what I believed was right. The doctor accepted the decision and said, "We need him to survive the night." I was shocked. Is my future husband about to die? The Lord gave me peace about it; this was the beginning of our story, not the end.

Thankfully, Andy was released from the hospital, and recovery at home took some time. He then said he had a confession to make. Uh oh, what now? Andy had prostate cancer that needed to be treated right away. Now, you may be thinking, "Ahh, that's why the Lord said don't let him go." Yes, that is it. This is about the time most women would run. Five kids and cancer? I was barely learning how to parent one kid. How could I manage six, knowing he could be terribly ill? I went home to discuss it with my daughter, and she said, "Mom, don't run. You can do this." It felt like Jesus was talking through her. It was like everything else the Lord was walking me through. The roses had thorns. It was all beautiful but challenging.

Meanwhile, the house I owned in Brentwood had been on the market since we had moved to Ventura County. It was more than a year, but it would not sell. Everything I had was sunk into that house. I made a promise to the Lord that if He would let the house sell, I would donate a portion of the funds to get Andy this state-of-the-art surgery for his cancer. Literally, within a week, we had a buyer for the house! With God's grace, Andy underwent the surgery, which was extremely successful. He is now cancer-free with no adverse side effects from the procedure.

Andy and I were married just three months after we met. Both of us knew the Lord was calling us into covenant with each other, and we would raise our children together. The transition was fast and came with its own challenges for all of us.

Admittedly, managing a large household does not come easily for me. My brother was rarely home growing up, so I lived much like a single child. I then spent my entire adult life living alone until my daughter was born. She and I lived in a huge home with rooms at opposite ends. I was barely there enough to be troubled by a child's ongoing needs. There was always someone around to clean, cook, and care for Zahra. Once I came into a relationship with Christ, three years later, she and I were in a blended family with six additional people.

God has a sense of humor, folks. He chose the most incredible way to teach me to love people as I loved myself. I had no concept of unconditional love until Andy and the kids came along. The Lord was taking me from the theoretical to the experiential. He needed me to live that Scripture from 1 Timothy 3. One cannot run a church or do ministry if you cannot even manage a household. At this point, I am not claiming to be Mrs. Brady from *The Brady Bunch*, but I have learned sacrifice, patience, and self-control. It's beautiful to feel like I am growing inside and my heart is expanding. Islam sought to stifle, but Jesus wanted to renew and regenerate.

THIRTEEN

Losing Dad

Before I came to saving faith in Christ, I depended on my father so intensely that I would cry just at the thought of him leaving this world. He was my anchor through the storms of life, always able to put me back on solid ground. My father had become a devout Muslim, and though my conversion was initially hard to accept, his love for my daughter and me never changed. He was still my biggest supporter, whether it was giving business advice for managing the ministry or watching my testimony on *The 700 Club*. As my relationship with the Lord grew in strength and I was blessed to start a blended family with my new husband, I began to experience what God commanded for a couple to leave their parents' homes and "become one flesh." I knew the Lord was calling me to "leave my parent's house" so I could grow in faith, but I never expected that my father would soon become gravely ill. In less than a year, a virulent strain of cancer metastasized across my father's body, and he left the earth.

While at the hospital, I passionately pleaded with my father to accept the free gift of salvation. He would always listen attentively and smile. After several of these conversations, I had peace that I had delivered the good news of the Gospel, and it was now between him and the Lord. Once the doctors determined the cancer was not treatable, we brought my father home to enjoy his remaining time surrounded by family. In just three days, with all the family present, my father passed. It happened so fast and so dramatically that none of us could emotionally prepare for what would happen next.

At his bedside, I saw the last breath leave his body, and almost instantly, I lost emotional connectivity to his flesh. I kissed his forehead and left the room. However, I was well aware that this time of passing of a soul, until the body is buried, can be pretty emotional for all my Muslim relatives. In Islam, there is no guarantee of eternal life or Heaven. The minute a person dies, they prepare for the judgment of god. A portion of the soul remains in the deceased, so great care is taken with the body. A ritual washing is performed within 24 hours; the body is wrapped in a white cloth with the face covered and then placed in the grave. It is believed that in the first evening, two very menacing angels appear to the deceased and question him about his faith and deeds, both good and bad. All this is accepted by faith and can be pretty traumatic for the family of the loved one. The next couple of days are spent praying for the deceased in hopes he would receive mercy, yet there is a lingering fear about what will happen in the afterlife. I could see the agony on their faces and the pain they were experiencing from that uncertainty. As the grief and fear swirled around the room, I was overwhelmed with gratitude for the surety of saving faith in Christ. The gift of salvation was suddenly so real to me. To be absent from the body is to be present with the Lord. I knew I would not need anyone to pray over my body because my trust in Jesus guaranteed me eternal life.

Over the next couple of days, preparations were made for the burial and the reception, including who would give a eulogy. I became so convicted about why we are commanded to preach the Gospel regardless of the personal cost. I desperately wanted my loved ones to avoid that fear of uncertainty for their own lives and wanted them to know that only Jesus could lift that burden. My father's reception was held in the Islamic center he founded over 20 years ago. The room was filled with more than 500 Muslim family members and friends, most of whom were male. I knew I had to testify to the power of Christ in my life and hopefully plant a seed of hope to whoever had ears to listen. Yet I was petrified about how angry some would be that I dared mention salvation through Christ.

Nonetheless, I walked to the podium, and the Lord gave me supernatural strength and courage. I spoke of the beautiful qualities my father taught me—patriotism, hard work, education, and unconditional love. I explained the love he demonstrated most profoundly by accepting my salvation through Christ. I told them how afraid I was to lose my earthly father, but I now had the love and protection of my Heavenly Father. Then I read:

> *"Even though I walk through the shadow of death I shall fear no evil for the Lord is with me. Surely your goodness and love will follow me all the days of my life, and I will dwell in the house of the Lord forever."*
>
> —*Psalm 23: 4,6*

Amazingly enough, all I heard from people afterward was how proud they were of my bravery, and some confessed they had also accepted Christ several years ago.

It has been three years since my father's passing, and I often try to witness to my mother about Christ. I pray every day for her salvation, but unfortunately, it does not seem to pique her interest. Recently, my mother dreamt of my father telling her she had to read the "green book." The "green book" is the Bible I left with her in Farsi, her native language. It demonstrated to me that God indeed hears our prayers and answers them. The only person my mother would ever listen to was my father, and a message came to her from beyond the grave. I may never know for sure whether my father accepted Christ in his remaining days, but that dream elevated my hopes I would see my father again. I do not know if that night at the mosque, someone in the audience was touched by Scripture and led to Christ. However, I do know that I have no regrets.

"This is eternal life, that they may know You, the only true God, and Jesus Christ whom You have sent."

—John 17:3

FOURTEEN

Seasons of Our Life

Now, *those* are words to live by!

Our lives consist of seasons. Some of them are our own private seasons, while others affect our families, our communities, and even a broader group of people. As those seasons come into our lives, what do they bring? How do *we* rise to meet them?

An ideal example of a season in life was the COVID pandemic that affected the entire world. It was easy to see the destruction in the pandemic—the negative ways our lives changed. However, for many of us, there were also positive influences at work during that season. I met the man of my dreams during COVID. Dating consisted of trips to fast food restaurants and the park, with long talks in the car. We got married under an oak tree. We felt so blessed to have good health and a courageous pastor who was changing lives with bold preaching. It was the best of times; it was the worst of times.

> *"Not by might nor by power, but by my Spirit, says the Lord Almighty."*
>
> —*Zechariah 4:6*

There will come a time in each of our lives when we may feel afraid and insecure. COVID brought that out in millions of people. It was especially striking in Christians because it tested everyone's faith and trust in God.

The pandemic was the first world crisis I experienced since becoming a follower of Jesus Christ. I had a whole new level of peace that I didn't have during other global scares I had experienced.

As a Muslim, there is an "End Times" doctrine that I passionately believed in, so I've been a "prepper" for many years. I have always kept a stock of non-perishable food, water, and medical supplies on hand. Even with my careful preparations, I was terrified at the thought of suffering through natural or man-made disasters.

Thanks to Christ, however, all that has changed for the better!

Following Christ has provided three things in particular that have protected me from fear.

Faith

As a follower of Christ, I have faith that the Holy Spirit within me—His Spirit—will guide and carry me through any storm. It provides an internal fortitude that keeps me calm and assures me that God is in control—just as He's always been.

My faith in Christ assures me that my steps are ordered and my destiny is preordained. If I obey His commands and listen to the guidance of the Holy Spirit, Christ will get me through whatever difficulties come my way. It does not guarantee I will not suffer, but it does guarantee I will not suffer in vain. Most importantly, I know how the story ends. It ends with eternity in Heaven next to Jesus. This life is but a vapor; in an instant, we are united with Him. This life becomes a distant memory. There will be no pain, no sickness. It is the promise of eternity that brings ultimate comfort.

Strength

"I discipline my body like an athlete, training it to do what it should. Otherwise, I fear that after preaching to others I myself might be disqualified."

—*1 Corinthians 9:27*

Amid the pandemic, the Lord impressed upon me that I needed to become physically stronger and able to defend myself. That might seem like common sense since my status as a former Muslim could lead to threats of death or grave bodily harm. Despite that, I was surprised by the Lord's instruction because, as Christians, I assumed we did not worry about war in the flesh. Nonetheless, I obeyed the instructions and started training with firearms and lifting weights.

I have come to understand that it was not necessarily about physical confrontation. As women, we often worry about personal security and feel almost defenseless if a man is not around to protect us. I highly recommend firearms training to any woman who is a survivor of abuse or who just feels insecure about being alone or unprotected. An amazing sense of inner comfort and strength comes from knowing how to defend oneself physically, if necessary.

I also believe that gaining bodily strength is essential in perilous times. I was entering menopause, and my muscles were getting weaker. I started weight training so I could perform basic household tasks, walk long distances, and lift heavy objects in an emergency. As world chaos increases, none of us wants to feel vulnerable. Physical strength has led to emotional and spiritual confidence as well. The Apostle Paul said he disciplined his body like an athlete to show he was worthy of his calling.

Spiritual Protection

"The Lord is my strength and my shield; my heart trusts in Him, and He helps me."

—Psalms 28:7

Though I felt inspired to become physically prepared, I also solidified my spiritual strength by regularly having communion at home. When the Jews were being rescued out of Egypt, the Lord told Moses that every family must put blood around their front doors so when the angel of death came to strike the male children of the cities, their boys would be safe. It was the blood of sacrifice that protected them. As believers in Christ, Jesus is our ultimate sacrifice and protection. At the last Passover, he ordered us to initiate the ceremony of Communion. We were to partake of his blood and body with the elements of wine and bread. He was the final sacrifice of blood as the price paid for the sins of all who believe in Him. It's the power of the Blood.

I bought communion capsules on Amazon, which are very convenient for anyone to use. At the end of the day, the blood of Christ is our ultimate protection. The Scripture assures us:

"Having now been justified by His blood, we shall be saved from wrath through Him."

—Romans 5:9

The elements of communion do not change or become the body and blood of the Lord in any way. The elements are symbols of His body and blood. Christ is present with us spiritually. It is not just the memory of Him that is present; He is in the midst of the congregation; He is present in our home. The emphasis is upon His presence within the worshiping body, not within the elements of the table. The believer communes with the Lord through the act of remembrance and worship.

Looking back on the pandemic, God was indeed at work in the hearts of His people. Who other than God could allow the entire world to be in captivity through something as small as a microscopic virus? God permitted the threat of death to hang over us, but the critical question was what God expected us to manifest through it. Our physical body was in bondage, but our spirit was free to worship and draw nearer to the Lord.

The pandemic is simply an example of a difficult season for many. Let's look at how we manage difficult seasons and situations with God's will in perspective. If God does not take us out of a tight spot, what is He bringing forth *in* us? There is always a purpose in our pain. The Apostle Paul wrote the book of Philippians from a prison cell. He did not know if he was going to live or die. Despite his seemingly desperate situation, Paul expressed uncertainty and confidence at the same time. He did not bother to describe the horrible circumstances in prison. Instead, he wanted to focus on the *fruit* of the situation.

He wrote:

> *"And because of my chains, most of the brothers and sisters have become confident in the Lord and dare all the more to proclaim the Gospel without fear."*
>
> —*Philippians 1:14.*

We all need to be bold enough to look at our lives in a similar way. We need to ask ourselves, *What is God pruning in me this season? What fruits does He desire me to cultivate?* Remember, what is happening *within* us is more important than what is happening *to* us.

> *"But the fruit of the Spirit is love, joy, peace, forbearance, kindness, goodness, faithfulness, gentleness, and self-control."*
>
> —*Galatians 5:22*

Those are the fruits He desires us to cultivate in every season—the good and the difficult.

In your current season, what do you hear God saying to you? Can you focus on what fruit He wants for your life rather than on the moment's frustration? What if this season of your life, which seems to be so difficult, is fast-forwarding you into the wisdom God wants for your life? Imagine the possibilities!

We are all equally ignorant as we contend with our current challenges. Nobody knows what lies ahead. God is the only one who knows the future—for each of us individually and the entire world. God's plans are a mystery, and faith does not negate uncertainty. In life, we can only control our individual emotional and spiritual focus. None of us needs to know how it all unfolds—only that God will be with us through it. It is a confidence that goes beyond knowledge.

The pain makes sense if we can focus on the transformation occurring in us. Pain without purpose is unbearable. We need to listen to what God is trying to teach us. Things concerning God usually do not happen overnight, though. That is why Jesus uses harvesting in so many of His parables. Growing fruit takes time. You need to prepare good soil that will be the best possible environment. You then need to plant that first seed, provide the appropriate water and fertilizer to nourish it, and you must give it *time*. The tree must grow before any fruit is produced. In various seasons, I sometimes feel covered in dirt—even occasionally buried—but I have hope in the Lord that He will help me make something beautiful out of it. Hope is a focus we all must *consciously* choose.

In Romans 8:23-25, Paul teaches us that transformation and redemption of our mortal bodies from sin and temptation is the promise we hold on to through the pain. If we had already experienced it completely, we would not have needed to hope for it. Nonetheless, there is a groaning and suffering that comes along with the waiting. I am so grateful for a God who prepares us for hardship. He does not pretend it will be easy. He teaches us to embrace it. He also promises to carry us through it. When we do not know what to pray, the Holy Spirit will pray for us.

"In the same way, the Spirit helps us in our weakness. We do not know what we ought to pray for, but the Spirit Himself intercedes for us through wordless groans. And He who searches our hearts knows the mind of the Spirit, because the Spirit intercedes for God's people in accordance with the will of God."

— *Romans 8: 26–27*

When we mess up or stumble, which is sure to happen, God will make it work to our advantage if we love Him and continue to follow His purpose.

FIFTEEN

Struggling With Holiness

"Dear friends, I urge you, as foreigners and exiles, to abstain from sinful desires, which wage war against your soul."

—*1 Peter 2:11*

As I was settling into life as a Christ follower, I knew Jesus was still doing a mighty work in me. Since Andy and I were married after only three months together. It was a whirlwind romance, and now we had to settle in as a blended family.

In just a few short years, I felt true happiness for the first time. I was married to a wonderful man. I gained a beautiful new family who filled my days with the adventures of four additional school-age children, one bonus adult young lady, and my precious daughter. We were surrounded by a great community and dedicated to civic engagement and local politics. We were blessed with good health and provisions to enjoy life's simple pleasures. The simple pleasures we enjoyed included alcohol. Though I knew the Lord had called me to sobriety, I rationalized that things were different now. I had a husband, and we could engage in social drinking together. I was so wrong. The occasional drink on the weekends turned into happy hour twice a week and weekend parties. Two drinks turned into five, and I felt miserable.

The pain of disobedience is probably the most challenging lesson of becoming God's disciple. When I first came to saving faith, it was easy to submerge myself in God's Word and practice holiness. When I decided to leave Islam, I was no longer in a relationship and had lost all my friends and family. All I had was Jesus, my devoted parents, and Zahra.

After about one year in the faith, the Lord put on my heart to consecrate myself, to be holy, and not give my heart to anyone except the man He would send. He made me give an oath that I would dedicate the marriage purely for His glory and that I *never* would turn back. I also vowed not to drink or consume any intoxicants or be driven back to worldly desires. All this inspiration came as I read the verses in 1 Samuel about Saul, the first King of the Israelites. When I was deep in prayer after reading, the Lord told me it was imperative to obey all His instructions, or the anointing could be eliminated. It was a very impactful moment in my prayer life and relationship with God. My mentor told me I would hear from God through His Scripture and this was definitely one of those times. I knew it was serious.

In this portion of Scripture, the Lord told Saul to kill all the Amalekites and not to leave anything behind. Instead of doing as he was told, he saved the best livestock and spared the king's life. Saul lost his anointing from God for this disobedience, and Samuel recited to him:

> *"Has the Lord as great a delight in burnt offerings and sacrifices, as in obeying the voice of the Lord? Behold, to obey is better than sacrifice, And to heed than the fat of rams…He who is the Glory of Israel does not lie or change His mind; for He is not a human being, that He should change his mind."*
>
> *—I Samuel 15:22,29*

I lived that way up until Andy and I were married. Now, with my new life, I tried to convince myself that I was doing enough by managing my new family and that partying was part of the plan. Alcohol is not forbidden in Christianity, so what was the problem? After all, a happy family environment is a big part of God's message to us as Christians. It sounds crazy, I know. I was not fooling myself or Jesus. I heard the still, soft voice of the Lord reminding me:

> *"Therefore, with minds that are alert and fully sober, set your hope on the grace to be brought to you when Jesus Christ is revealed at His coming. As obedient children, do not conform to the evil desires you had when you lived in ignorance. But just as He who called you is holy, so be holy in all you do."*
>
> *—1 Peter 1:13-15*

I know many of you who read this will think my prohibition of alcohol is a remnant of my Islamic faith, but that is not the case. I could not manage to drink alcohol and remain "sober-minded." I could not practice holiness if happy hour was a fixture in my week. At first, I rationalized that the voice was just the Type-A overachiever in me wanting to do more. It was easy to disregard at first, but the guilt was eating me alive.

Nonetheless, I continued in my rebellion. The Lord was prompting me, and I ignored it. I ignored *Him*.

Then suddenly, Andy and I received some devastating news that literally brought me to my knees in remorse. We were being evicted from our home in 60 days. The housing market was terrible, and we had no clue where we would go. I instantly knew the Lord was disciplining me. The Lord had commanded specific actions, but I had not obeyed, and I knew it. I had neglected Jesus Christ, my first love. I could hear His words:

> *"Why do you call me 'Lord, Lord,' and not do what I tell you?"*
>
> *—Luke 6:46*

Grace is such incredible mercy that covers the life of a believer. However, as the Bible says:

> *"Without holiness, no one will see the Lord."*
>
> —*Hebrews 12:14*

Like me, you may reason that you have not committed the big sins— adultery, fornication, murder. It's important to note that the Lord isn't *only* concerned with the biggies. We must put aside *all* forms of disobedience, including what He personally calls us to.

Wait, didn't the Lord pay the price of our sins when He suffered in Gethsemane and hung on the cross? Yes, but that doesn't let us off the hook. The Lord wants our lives to reflect His presence so He can work *in* and *through* us.

God disciplines us in a corrective way when we disobey. It is never out of malice or spite. He disciplines us for our good so we can share in His holiness. That might be hard to accept at first. Discipline hurts.

> *"They disciplined us for a little while as they thought best; but God disciplines us for our good, in order that we may share in His holiness. No discipline seems pleasant at the time, but painful. Later on, however, it produces a harvest of righteousness and peace for those who have been trained by it."*
>
> —*Hebrews 12:10–11*

The hardest battle is often *within* us, not *against* other people. Therefore, we must be on our guard. In these troubled times, we are called to even greater submission. In our obedience, in surrendering to His plan, we reflect that Christ lives in us, which will draw others toward Him. We are told:

> *"Live such good lives among the pagans that, though they accuse you of doing wrong, they may see your good deeds and glorify God on the day He visits us."*
>
> —*1 Peter 2:12*

Nearly a century ago, British evangelist Smith Wigglesworth said something that still rings true today: "The reason the world is not seeing Jesus is that Christian people are not filled with Jesus." We are not trying to win a popularity contest; we know we will be hated for His name's sake. What we *are* trying to accomplish is that our actions draw the lost and brokenhearted to the goodness Christ can offer.

Like so many other great men and women of the Bible, Peter loved God but failed miserably to demonstrate that love at first. Peter was the rock on which the Lord would build His church, but he also denied the Lord three times within moments of the Lord's capture.

Peter was not the only one who struggled with disobedience. The prophet Abraham left paganism to follow God and was the father of all nations. Yet, he pretended his wife was his sister to avoid the wrath of a king. The great warrior and statesman, King David, a man after God's own heart, stole someone's wife and killed her husband to cover it up.

As Christians, we have a *submission* crisis, not an *identity* crisis. Though the discipline I suffered was painful, it held an important lesson for me from Jesus. It was not for me to rationalize whether His calling for me was necessary. He was calling me to obedience. I should have listened. I was learning that my plans had to take a backseat to His plan for me.

In the book of Romans, the Apostle Paul testifies:

> *"For if you live according to the flesh, you will die; but if by the Spirit you put to death the deeds of the body, you will live."*
>
> —*Romans 8:13*

It may seem hard to believe that dying to self gives true life. That's not our choice, yet it is what the Word teaches us. In hard times, we may want to turn inward to protect ourselves, but that is not our calling. When we obey and avoid sin, we demonstrate good character, show perfect love to the family of believers, and even show love to our enemies since our behavior is our witness. We behave this way in honor of Jesus dying on the cross for us. We are called to follow in the footsteps of our Savior.

Remember that the book of Revelation begins with the Lord's rebuke to the churches, to the body of believers in Christ Jesus. He admonishes them for being lukewarm, spoiled by riches, and sexually immoral. He warns the believers to overcome the enemy's temptations and endure until He returns, or there will be consequences. Salvation happens in an instant, but sanctification takes a lifetime. Even when we disobey—and we *will* disobey—we must get back on track, following God. He will then restore us. I am grateful that just like He did for the great prophets of old, my God forgives and redeems those who turn to Him in repentance, including me.

Paul wrote to the Hebrews:

> "My child, don't make light of the Lord's discipline and don't give up when He corrects you. For the Lord disciplines those He loves, and He punishes each one he accepts as His child."
>
> —Hebrews 12:5–6

Anyone who has experienced the Lord's chastisement knows how difficult it can be. The chastisement indicates His love and desire for goodness in our lives. He is not trying to deprive us of fun; He wants us to experience what real joy feels like.

As we commit to moving forward in obedience, what of all the times when we disobeyed, maybe even intentionally? Thankfully, part of the good news of the Gospel is that Jesus Christ paid the price for our sins so we can be in right standing with God. Without His substitutional atonement, we would owe that price to God. So, our part is what we are told in Scripture:

> "If we confess our sins, He is faithful and just and will forgive us our sins and purify us from all unrighteousness."
>
> —1 John 1:9

Our part, then, is to pray, repent, and share with Him the sorrow we feel over disobedience.

Once we accept Jesus as our Lord and Savior, we are a new creation. However, our old habits, thoughts, patterns, behaviors, and spiritual bondage remain with us until we allow the Holy Spirit to regenerate us. There is a divine partnership between what we control in our flesh and what God is trying to do within us. We cannot continue following our lusts and old vices and expect transformation. Like anything good in life, hard work must follow.

Repentance is a process that involves calling to mind our old sins—infidelity, promiscuity, drug use, alcohol abuse, or whatever our past wrongdoing may be—and then turning away from those actions. The Greek word is *Metanoia*, which literally means to turn away from. It is a process we must do continually. You do not have to suffer the pains of the disobedience that marred your life before you accepted Jesus Christ as your Savior.

Simply bring those things to the feet of Jesus. When you do, He will cleanse you of all unrighteousness.

SIXTEEN

The Public School Challenges

Andy and I are raising five school-aged children at all public school levels—elementary, middle, and high school. Like many parents, we learned the bizarre concepts they were being exposed to by listening in on their Zoom calls during COVID. It was not long before we realized parents needed to be more aware of what they were being taught. It was up to us to protect our children from the dangerous influences of teachers and administrators who do not share our values.

Dangerous influences?

Yes. That may seem exaggerated, but it is true. It was all there, and it continued to proliferate without our diligent effort.

I'm not talking about gangs that have set up shop in high schools. Nor am I talking about the kids who make a living by selling drugs to their classmates. I'm not even talking about the random active shooter who manages to get into a school before gunning down teachers, students, and members of the administration.

Sadly, all those things exist in our schools to some degree. Stringent measures must be taken to protect students and faculty members from the hazards they pose. Yet there is a more insidious threat to our kids in public schools—indoctrination that is as dangerous as sending them into the wolves' den.

I'm talking about the evil forces that feed not on the flesh but on the soul.

I'm going to use California schools as the example since they are most familiar to me; however, this is happening across the nation. These insidious principles are seeping into almost all public schools. Without concerned parents, these damaging influences go unchecked.

Over several years, California Governor Gavin Newsom's popularity seemed to progressively erode. His policies were losing favor, and citizens were weary of his inability to correct serious problems throughout the state. An impressive grassroots campaign to recall the governor was launched and gained widespread support.

A special recall election was held. Despite the extraordinary campaign by those who wanted him out of office, Californians were unsuccessful in their effort to recall Governor Newsom.

He was allowed to stay in office and exact revenge on his opponents through several mandates targeting our most vulnerable population—children.

Newsom signed into law California Assembly Bill 1184, the medical information confidentiality bill. The bill allows *minors*—children under the age of 18—to keep "sensitive services" confidential from whoever holds their insurance, which is generally their parents.

To avoid any confusion, here's what that means. Your minor child can be given contraception (even an implanted device), have an abortion, and even undergo gender reassignment surgery *without you being told a thing about it or giving your permission.*

You read that right. Your 15-year-old daughter could have an abortion, and you wouldn't have to consent to the procedure. In fact, you'd never even know the abortion had been done.

Your 12-year-old son could go through all the hormonal and therapeutic measures to change his gender characteristics to that of a female without your knowledge or permission.

This law not only affects parental rights over their minor children but can also create financial burdens for parents, who are obligated to pay for the services done at a facility without their knowledge. In other words, even though you never consented to or even knew about the abortion your 15-year-old daughter had, you will pay the bill.

Soon after that, Newsom signed into law California Assembly Bill 101, which states that all high school graduates must have at least one semester of ethnic studies to graduate. On its face, an ethnic studies curriculum that provides a well-rounded perspective on people from different cultures seems like a good thing. However, it is often a smokescreen for teaching Critical Race Theory, which is dangerously anti-American and antisemitic.

Lastly, in what many consider the breaking point, Governor Newsom announced that COVID vaccines would be mandatory for in-person learning once full FDA approval was granted in July 2022. Newsom wanted to add the COVID vaccine to the list of other vaccines required by law for any student to attend any school in the state. California has one of the most stringent vaccination laws because it does *not* allow exemptions based on personal or religious beliefs and prohibits most medical exceptions.

In my district, Placentia Yorba Linda Unified, hundreds of concerned parents attended a school board meeting, hoping to sway the school board into taking a stand against these measures. The overwhelming opinion of parents who spoke at the meeting, which lasted until midnight, was that these actions are antithetical to our values as a community.

Our district was not alone in its disapproval. Many parents and students staged walkouts across California to protest the vaccine mandates in particular. Across the United States, parents were standing up against the state's targeting of our children. Many felt the best solution was to homeschool their children, and they were pulling their kids out of public education in unprecedented numbers.

For Christians, all these regulations go to the core of our beliefs on pre-marital sex, gender, racial equality, and our right to make medical decisions on behalf of our own family. However, we need to ask ourselves, is turning thousands of parents into stay-at-home teachers and isolating our kids from the rest of society the best solution as Christ followers? We need to face the fact that when we turn our schools over to those who seek to permanently remove God from the public square and teach a neo-Marxist philosophy to whoever is left behind, it sends the message that we are not willing to fight for what we believe is right.

On the other hand, we have a responsibility as parents to protect and raise our kids in the ways of the Lord until they can defend themselves morally and intellectually. The reality of public education is that our kids will spend eight hours a day under those influences and maybe a couple of hours under ours. If Christian worldview training is not integrated as a part of a child's education, it is much less likely to happen.

Therein lies the difficult paradox. We should not abandon our schools, but we cannot use our kids as missionaries in hostile territory. Regardless of where our children go to school or if that phase of life has passed, we have a responsibility to be involved in the public schools to ensure they are not emotionally or spiritually abusing children in our communities. We are taxpayers, and therefore, it IS our business!

We need to expand programs like "Bring your Bible to School Day" and Christian student clubs on lower school campuses in addition to colleges. We need to publicly and fervently support believing Christians who run for their school boards and city councils across America.

The only way we can stem the tide of demonic influences flooding our cities and the nation is to follow Christ and the examples God has given us throughout humanity. Remember the prophet Daniel, who refused the king's decree to stop worshipping God. Remember the Apostle Paul, who boldly stood up to the Romans who threatened to kill him for preaching. God teaches us to defend the truth of His Word despite the consequences.

> *"Blessed are you when people insult you, persecute you, and falsely say all kinds of evil against you because of me. Rejoice and be glad, because great is your reward in Heaven, for in the same way, they persecuted the prophets who were before you."*
>
> *—Matthew 5:11–12*

Many of us were horrified to watch the total surrender of our values on the world stage when the United States unilaterally withdrew from Afghanistan. If all Bible-believing Christians pull their kids out of public school and refuse to fight for the School Boards, isn't that sending a similar message?

We live in perilous times, and there is a lot at stake. No parent takes the well-being of their children lightly, so emotions are running high. For some, homeschooling and private Christian schools are not financially possible. There will be nothing easy about this battle. Yet, if we equip our children to withstand the difficulty of being believers when it is increasingly unpopular, then we are preparing them for real life in the years to come. Hopefully, they will take that strength and courage into adulthood to witness to others what it means to follow Christ.

In our immediate family, we ended up having to pull my daughter out of public high school to study online. The negative influences of peers and a failure to properly supervise the campus made it too dangerous to stay. I share this with you because our fight to win back public schools is fierce. Some kids are tougher than others and can withstand the pressures to conform. Others need greater attention and protection until they mature and can thrive independently. Out of our five children, one was unable to fight it on her own.

In some instances, creating a safe environment for all children may take years. However, the way it is now, we need to evaluate each case to see how best to raise our kids in a world where the deck is stacked against them.

PART 3

RELIGION
AND RELATIONSHIP

"And we know and rely on the love God has for us. God is love. Whoever lives in love lives in God, and God in them."

—*1 John 4:16*

SEVENTEEN

Leaving Allah, Meeting Jesus

At this point, you are likely wondering *how* I could intellectually and emotionally detach myself from a religion to which I had been so fervently devoted throughout most of my adult life. It was the religion of all my ancestors, my parents, and everyone I loved.

Right off the top, there were several reasons why I decided it was time to leave Islam.

The first one had more to do with me than with Islam. As I reflected on my life, I believed that I had been fighting evil spirits from the very beginning. I remember being on the playground in Culver City, California, and taunting the other kids to do something shocking. I mean *really* shocking. The irony is that I was the only one who ultimately agreed to do it. Something dark and sinister was constantly drawing me towards actions and people that would do me harm. It felt like there was no "inner voice" in me that restrained my actions. I did nearly any wicked thing that popped into my head. By the time I was a teenager, that destructiveness was wearing me down. I hated it so I turned to Islam. However, I quickly realized the forces in my Muslim life were pretty much the same. There was no peace, just oppression.

Second, some specific parts of Islam were always a problem for me. The most significant of those was that Islam did not guide me toward a direct connection to god. Without that connection, I felt like I was flying blind. In Islam, the believer is never meant to hear from god directly. It was beneath the god of the universe to speak to lowly creation. That left a raw and troubling void in my heart and soul that nothing could fill.

Third, all the rituals and rules frankly did not work. I did not mature or grow as a person. I did not become a better or kinder person as a result of the endless religious practices. It just left me angry, bitter, and tired.

When I compare that to the three foundational principles I learned about being a Christ follower, the choice was obvious.

First, salvation is a free gift.

> *"For it is by grace you have been saved, through faith—and this is not from yourselves, it is the gift of God."*
>
> *—Ephesians 2:8*

It is a simple truth my heart quickly embraced. Something in me instinctively knew that to be true because striving for a god's forgiveness never worked.

In Islam, you never really know if your good deeds are enough to qualify you to enter god's heaven. Islam teaches that on the Day of Judgment, god will decide if you were *good enough* to get there. That terrified me. What if I had committed one big sin that he simply could not forgive despite my hundred acts of obedience? It was very unsettling to live day-to-day wondering whether I would spend eternity in hellfire.

As I immersed myself more deeply into understanding Christianity, I learned that God would guarantee a place in His eternal Heaven if I put my trust in Christ as God incarnate. I needed to accept that Jesus was God wrapped in flesh, who came to earth, died on the cross, and then rose again from the grave to pay for *my* sins. It is so comforting to believe that God loves me so completely that He would give His only Son so that I could be saved.

My daughter said it best, "Well, *that's* a no-brainer!" Why would I *not* accept that free gift of salvation?"

As a Muslim, I accepted that Jesus was born of a virgin birth, ascended to Heaven when His ministry on Earth was finished, and will descend back to Earth from Heaven in the last days to defeat the Antichrist. Since He possesses those miraculous qualities, it is actually quite logical that He is God incarnate.

Second, the one true God is love.

God does not hate us or do things out of spite. He is just. That means the price of every sin must be paid. The solution? He gave His only Son to pay the price for all our sins so we can be forgiven and have eternal life while still meeting the demands of justice.

The rest is about unconditional love.

In the more than 20 years I spent as a devout Muslim, I *never* heard god referred to as being love or as commanding us to love others. I was taught that god was merciful (the Arabic word *rahman*) and benevolent (the Arabic word *rahim*). I suppose you could stretch that concept to mean that god is extremely merciful or nurturing like a parent, but it is still not the word *love*.

So, I was worshipping and sacrificing for a god who did not tell me He loved me?

How depressing.

Compare that to the Bible, God's infallible and living Word. It's right there, in black and white, in His own words. He says He *is* love. He expresses His love for each one of us over and over again. There's no mistaking it. No ambiguity.

He is the originator and fulfiller of everything we know and experience about love. Jesus also teaches us that the *most* important commandment for us as believers is to love God and love other people:

> *"Love the Lord your God with all your heart and with all your soul and with all your mind and with all your strength. The second is this: 'Love your neighbor as yourself.' There is no commandment greater than these."*
>
> *—Mark 12:30–31*

The foundation of our faith is love. To me, this is one of the most beautiful and enriching aspects of Christianity. Being loved unconditionally and loving others the same way has brought me extraordinary joy. Unconditional love has improved my relationships beyond my wildest expectations.

Third, I will receive the Holy Spirit to live inside of me forever.

> *"If you love Me, keep My commands. And I will ask the Father, and He will give you another advocate to help you and be with you forever—the Spirit of truth. The world cannot accept Him, because it neither sees Him nor knows Him. But you know Him, for He dwells with you and will be in you. I will not leave you as orphans; I will come to you."*
>
> *—John 14:15–18*

That's not all. I also learned:

> *"When He, the Spirit of truth, comes, He will guide you into all the truth; He will not speak on His own, He will speak only what He hears; and He will tell you what is yet to come."*
>
> *—John 16:13*

Jesus tells believers that the Holy Spirit, the third member of the trinity (the third reality of God), is inside each of us! I no longer had to rely on another person's opinion about God's plan for me. I no longer wandered aimlessly, wondering about God's plan for my life. God would tell me directly. That means that the Holy Spirit inside me would direct my path. If I listened closely enough, I could avoid making misguided choices that I might make if I were left to my own desires or thoughts. Receiving the Holy Spirit and communion with Him radically transformed how I make decisions and has led to the most awe-inspiring experiences of my life.

I could go on endlessly describing how these three principles have changed my life forever, but I hope this much helps you appreciate why I have so boldly and wholeheartedly become a Christ-follower. I pray that you will consider these principles and will ask God to reveal His reality to you. I firmly believe He will meet you where you are!

In addition to these three main principles of faith in Christ, there is another reason I left Islam. Before my salvation through Christ, I spent more than two decades trying to defeat Islamic radicalization. I built evidence-based programs across the United States and around the world, partnering with law enforcement and communities to hopefully prevent young men or women from committing ideologically motivated violence. Even though I felt proud of all I had accomplished, I had to admit I never solved the problem. No matter what any of us *experts* did, the terrorists multiplied.

I kept doing the same things over and over and expecting different results—something that some experts define as *insanity*. After a while, it was exhausting, and I felt worthless. So, I simply stopped doing it.

Islam left me miserable. Following Christ was enriching and inspiring.

In Romans, Paul appeals to God's promises to Abraham as evidence that there has never been a distinction among people who believe His message by faith. God's plan all along has been that this message would bless all nations through faith in Jesus. It doesn't matter whether you come from the law of the Jews, from Paganism, or Islam. Once you put your trust in Christ, we are all the same. We are all reborn as children of God.

> *"It was not through the law that Abraham and his offspring received the promise that he would be heir of the world, but*

through the righteousness that comes by faith. For if those who depend on the law are heirs, faith means nothing, and the promise is worthless, because the law brings wrath. And where there is no law there is no transgression. Therefore, the promise comes by faith, so that it may be by grace and may be guaranteed to all Abraham's offspring—not only to those who are of the law but also to those who have the faith of Abraham. He is the father of us all."

—Romans 4:13–16

Adam brought sin into the world, but Jesus brought a gift. With Adam, death multiplied because all have sinned; with Jesus, grace multiplied as God's gift of forgiveness was offered to everyone. We are told:

"For just as through the disobedience of the one man the many were made sinners, so also through the obedience of the one man the many will be made righteous."

—Romans 5:19

A revolutionary personal experience with Jesus Christ can empower you to be free of that domination and reach your true potential—not just professionally but emotionally and personally in your relationship with yourself and your Creator.

An encounter with Jesus Christ, who is both the son of man and the son of God, radically turns our situation on its head. He paid the ultimate price for your freedom with His own blood. He promises that faith in Him sets you free from the burden of sin, death, hell, and the grave. We are born twice and die once. With faith in Him, you are guaranteed to receive the indwelling of the Holy Spirit, the third person of the Trinity, who communicates directly on your behalf with God, our Father. The Holy Spirit living inside of you is your Counselor, comforter, and intercessor when you are too broken or weak to even say what your needs are.

EIGHTEEN

Who Is Jesus?

"Regarding His Son, who as to His earthly life was a descendant of David and who through the Spirit of holiness was appointed the Son of God in power by His resurrection from the dead: Jesus Christ our Lord."

—Romans 1:3–4

One of the most controversial aspects of being a follower of Christ is also one of the greatest: Jesus Christ is the Son of God.

Many people have a hard time grasping what that simple reality really means. Islam wants to accuse Christians of being polytheists, but that's not what the Scripture says at all.

The truth is beautiful and exquisite. There is only *one* God, and He manifests in three separate beings: the Father, the Son (Jesus Christ), and the Holy Spirit, who does not have a body of flesh and resides in *all* believers simultaneously.

Let me state it with a little different perspective. You probably accept that God created the whole universe in six days, representing either six 24-hour periods or a greater length of time. It includes all planets, solar systems, vegetation, animals, insects, fish, birds, and mankind. If you can accept that, it should not be too difficult to accept that He can manifest Himself in as many ways as He chooses—especially to make Himself known to humans, who are the crown of His creation and made in His image.

God provides one of the most eloquent descriptions of the Son, Jesus Christ, in Colossians:

> *"The Son is the image of the invisible God, the firstborn over all creation. For in Him all things were created: things in Heaven and on earth, visible and invisible, whether thrones or powers or rulers or authorities; all things have been created through Him and for Him...For God was pleased to have all His fullness dwell in Him, and through Him to reconcile to Himself all things, whether things on earth or things in Heaven, by making peace through His blood, shed on the cross."*
>
> *—Colossians 1:15–16, 19–20*

In the first chapter of Romans, the Apostle Paul affirms the dual nature of Christ and how he is simultaneously entirely human and entirely God. The human aspect of Jesus was created, but the divine nature within Him, which was God, is eternal and uncreated. He is 100 percent both in one.

> *"[Jesus] Was born a descendant of David according to the flesh, who was declared Son of God in power according to the Holy Spirit by the resurrection from the dead of Jesus Christ our Lord."*
>
> *—Romans 1:3–4*

In another passage, God foreshadows the arrival of Jesus by saying:

> *"Unto us a Child is born, unto us a Son is given."*
>
> *—Isaiah 9:6*

Therefore, the part of Christ that is Son of the Father is not born to the Father; He is given. Like the Father Himself, that aspect of His being is entirely uncreated. However, that uncreated divine nature was "wrapped" in flesh and was born on earth through the virgin Mary to save humanity from the penalty of its sins.

When Mary questioned the notion that she would give birth to a child even though she was chaste and had never been with a man, the angel of God tried to calm her fears and answer her altogether logical questions by explaining to Mary, the dual nature of her child:

> *"And the angel answered and said to her, 'The Holy Spirit will come upon you, and the power of the Most High will overshadow you. Therefore, also the one to be born will be called holy, the Son of God.'"*
>
> *—Luke 1:35*

Despite the elaborate detail of Jesus's duality, Paul subtly warns us not to think Jesus's human nature means we should worship mortal things. In fact, quite the opposite is true! He teaches us that no mortal thing can ever fill the place of the immortal God and that focusing on material things is the kind of foolishness that eventually leads only to sin and death (see Romans 1:22–23).

Scripture provides a great example. Paul seems to mock the Jews for assigning Godlike qualities to foolish things like the golden calf. In doing so, he warns us not to worship worldly things like money or fame. We should never think worldly objects or idols can answer our prayers or supply our wants and needs. He also intimates that no being of any kind *other than God* is worthy of worship. Humans are tempted to try to fill the hollow places inside us with these "beings"— the worldly things that surround us and tempt us. Yet, Paul makes it clear that they never can fill the void that only a relationship with Christ/God can fill.

Paul goes on to say that if we are willing to sacrifice such an important truth as the supremacy of God by engaging in idol worship, then the lesser truths aren't far behind. Paul's approach is less of a moral judgment and more of an observation regarding the natural consequences of human decisions.

Human beings end up tolerating all sorts of emotional degradation in abusive and co-dependent relationships because we have already rejected the primacy of God in our lives. We trade in our dependence on God alone for reliance on a spouse or loved one and expect that person to fill the void in our lives. Inevitably, they will fall short. The only one who never falls short is God.

Wholeness and true contentment can come only from a relationship with God through Christ. We are not seeking a religion with a set of rules that make up an endless set of actions we must perform. I despise religion in that sense. Coming into a relationship with Jesus is about trusting Him with your life—in this world and the next. It is about emulating His character—the compassion and the love He showered on humanity without measure. I pursue holiness out of love for Him and what He sacrificed for me. I do not do it because I fear Hell. The guilt and shame are gone. All that remains is love.

NINETEEN

Three Tests that Prove the Bible Is God's Infallible, Living Word

"For we did not follow cunningly devised fables when we made known to you the power and coming of our Lord Jesus Christ but were eyewitnesses of His majesty."

—2 Peter 1:16

I accepted Jesus Christ as my Lord and Savior after having a profound supernatural experience of hearing Him call my name. Though I was listening to many sermons and praying, this encounter made His reality undeniable for me. I was in desperate need of a direct relationship with God, and He revealed Himself.

Jesus answered my call. It was that clear and convincing. I could never ignore it or go back to what I was before that moment.

As absolutely precious as that experience was to me, I am very aware that not every believer will have a similar encounter with God. Regardless of how you come to saving faith in Christ, every believer should be able to objectively articulate why the Bible is God's infallible, living Word.

If we define and communicate why the Bible is authentic, our faith is defensible beyond the experiential. We can build our confidence in the Bible and provide objective evidence to draw people to Him.

How can we independently defend that the Bible is the Word of God? Take, for example, Peter's writings as an eyewitness to Jesus's life and miracles. What he wrote was based on inspiration from God through the Holy Spirit.

Peter wrote:

> *"For we were not making up clever stories when we told you about the powerful coming of our Lord Jesus Christ. We saw his majestic splendor with our own eyes."*

—2 Peter 1:16

You may be thinking, it's all well and good to have the word of ancient Apostles who claimed to be eyewitnesses, but how can you, I, or anyone else verify the authenticity of the Bible?

Impact Video Ministries did an excellent job of outlining how to evaluate the Apostles' assertions and the Bible's integrity. Their video is online and provides excellent ways for us to verify the Bible.[1]

First: The Honesty Test

It is very significant when a historical account includes disparaging details about the author. Why? It indicates that the author is more concerned about telling the truth than telling an amazing story about himself. Otherwise, he would have changed the facts to make himself look better—and what results is a lie.

Look closely at what the Bible tells us. Gospel writers Matthew and Mark tell us that Jesus called Peter Satan when he argued with Jesus over his coming death. Matthew, Mark, and Luke admit that Jesus was upset that the disciples fell asleep at the entrance to Gethsemane,

---

[1] Why Should I Trust the Bible? | IMPACT Whiteboard Video (youtube.com)

despite His repeated requests that they stay awake and watch with Him as He was in prayer. All four Gospel writers explain how the disciples abandoned Jesus when He was arrested. They all denied knowing Jesus and even hid after He died. It does not paint a rosy picture of these men, does it?

Furthermore, almost all the disciples died gruesome deaths. Why would they be willing to die for a lie? They could have escaped by renouncing their faith, but they didn't. They were so committed to relaying the truth that they were willing to die for it. That alone is a real indication that they were being honest in their reports and testimonies, which are recorded in the Bible.

Second: The Historical Accuracy of the Bible

One way to test the historical accuracy of the Bible is the "time gap"—how long after the actual events was the first copy written?

Handwritten documents of historical or spiritual significance are referred to as *manuscripts* before they are made into copies and reproduced. The manuscripts about Caesar were written 1,000 years after his life; those about Plato were written about 1,200 years after his death. The first biography of Alexander the Great was written 400 years after he lived, but no one doubts his existence.

The New Testament was written *only 50 years* after Jesus's death, making the time gap between Jesus's death and the record of His life far less than that of any other major event in ancient history.

When you compare the number of original manuscripts about Jesus's life, original manuscripts about the other historical figures do not even come close. Everything written about Caesar is contained in only ten manuscripts. Seven manuscripts contained everything written about Plato. But the New Testament has more than 24,633 original manuscripts! The closest to that is Homer's *Iliad*, which includes only 643 manuscripts.

No one contests the historical facts of Caesar and Plato. Their presence is widely accepted throughout the world and in history. Yet some still contest the authenticity of the Bible, even though its records about Christ far exceed any other.

Another test of the Bible's historical accuracy is the prophetic Scripture about the nation of Israel and its rebirth (see Isaiah 66:7-9), as well as the coming of Jesus Christ[2]. The Bible covers the entire span of humanity, beginning with Adam and Eve in the Garden, and tells of events in the future with perfect accuracy. In fact, critics are often shocked by its precision that they claim parts of the Old Testament had to have been written after the fact. However, this is not so.

The criticism of Christianity I hear most often from Muslims is that the Bible has been corrupted, though no one can ever provide the factual evidence to back up this assertion. The discovery of the Dead Sea Scrolls[3] finally put this notion to rest. Dated from around 200 B.C. to A.D. 68, the scrolls are more than *1,000 years older* than any manuscripts of the Hebrew Old Testament that were in existence before their discovery. Given their age and close similarity with the text used in the Bible from the tenth century, we have an *objective* basis for determining that the Biblical text used in our modern copies of the Old Testament is accurate. This means the Scriptures referring to Jesus and recreating Israel in a day (see Isaiah 66:7-9) were all written thousands of years ago.

Third: The Corroboration Test

What other historical materials confirm or deny the facts in the Bible? Nine non-Christian sources mention Jesus within 100 years of His death, and 33 additional sources are written by Christians, creating 42 records in total.

Caesar, whose existence is totally unquestioned, appears in only ten records written within 100 years of *his* death.

---

[2] https://www.gotquestions.org/Old-Testament-Christ.html
[3] https://lifehopeandtruth.com/bible/is-the-bible-true/proof-2-dead-sea-scrolls/

Jesus's life, His crucifixion, His reappearance through resurrection, and His ascension back to Heaven were corroborated four times as much, yet people still deny that He died and rose again.

The Bible dramatically passes all three tests. Even the skeptic should take pause and consider that the Bible is the Living Word of God. Share the good news of eternal life and forgiveness of sins through faith in Christ, not just because you feel it is right but because there is undeniable, irrefutable evidence that God sent His only Son to save us.

By its definition, religion is man's attempt to reach or find God. In the Bible, God cries out, inviting—even pleading with us—to meet Him face to face, to be in a relationship with Him that goes way beyond a set of rules of religion. The Bible is one of the ways God communicates to each and every one of us that we are loved.

In fact, the Bible is God's love letter to each of us. It is a love letter that serves as our first and greatest source of inspiration. When we read God's words in the Bible, the Holy Spirit can inspire our hearts with thoughts uniquely designed to change our lives. The Bible tells the story of humanity like no other book we have access to. It is not merely a history book. It is the only book of history in which God speaks directly to each and every one of us. Therein lies its power. It is the only history book where God repeatedly professes His love for us.

Make the Bible an important part of your life because, through His Word, God sends His message of love to all of humanity and for all time.

TWENTY

Casting Out Demons

Amid spiritual darkness and worldwide financial uncertainty, we are witnessing an extraordinary move of God. Whether it's the revival that began at Asbury University in Kentucky, the massive popularity of the *Jesus Revolution* film, or the mainstreaming of demonic deliverance, everyday people are learning about the power of the Holy Spirit. Not only are they hearing the Gospel, but society is witnessing the supernatural transformation that occurs from a radical encounter with the Risen Savior.

As a result of the sudden popularity of spiritual gifts, social media is filled with passionate arguments over the Biblical authority of Christians to heal the sick and cast out demons. The most controversial aspect of this is whether Christians can be demon-possessed. I have spent many hours learning the perspectives of respected scholars on this issue to better understand my faith journey. Though I cannot offer a professional conclusion, here are some lessons I have learned along the way.

When I came to saving faith in Christ, I was breaking with patterns of my ancestors that dated back thousands of years. There were countless generations of idol worship, polygamy, sexual immorality, and debauchery—without the blood of Jesus anywhere to be found. I had no idea whether these habits were passed down to me genetically like heart disease, or spiritually through demonic strongholds. However, I knew that complete regeneration required my conscious commitment to walking in Christ's victory for me at the cross.

The process began with prayer and repentance.

> *"If we confess our sins, He is faithful and just and will forgive us our sins and purify us from all unrighteousness."*
>
> *—1 John 1:9*

Without bringing it to Christ, the actions that trapped me in sin continued to plague my mind and affect my behavior. I had to lay each one at the feet of Jesus, believing in His purification, while praying for the Holy Spirit to do the rest. Without belief, repentance, and the power of the Holy Spirit, there is no victory. Yet, the process of restoration and regeneration took time. We do a disservice to our fellow brothers and sisters when we do not acknowledge the spiritual warfare it takes for some believers to break those strongholds. I am so grateful for the compassionate prayer warriors who walked alongside me to encourage and keep me accountable.

> *"Confess your trespasses to one another, and pray for one another, that you may be healed. The effective, fervent prayer of a righteous man avails much."*
>
> *—James 5:16*

In the Church, everyone acknowledges the importance of praying for others, but it gets testy when someone needs deliverance from demonic oppression. Personally, I do not believe any other being can inhabit a Christian whom the Holy Spirit possesses.

"Do you not know that your bodies are temples of the Holy Spirit, who is in you, whom you have received from God? You are not your own; you were bought at a price. Therefore, honor God with your bodies."

—*1 Corinthians 6:19-20*

I cannot envision a situation where He allows a roommate in that temple. However, I do think the Scriptures teach that believers can be demonized or afflicted by evil forces, or we would not be putting on the armor of God every day (Ephesians 6: 10-18). When we read the account of the demoniac living in the cemetery in Mark 5:1-20, the demons recognized the authority of Christ, and they begged Him to let them enter the pigs instead of the abyss. After the man was free of his demonic torment, Jesus told him to tell the others what happened. Two audiences needed to hear that Jesus held authority over the demons: the demons and the man.

We find a similar story in Mark 9:14-27 when the father brings Jesus his demon-possessed son, a crowd gathers, and then He casts the demon out. Again, His authority is demonstrated to both demons and men. Christ passes that authority to members of His Body, the Church, so our authority is a derived one. Believers cast out demons in the name of Jesus Christ, not by any power we possess outside of Him.

So, whether that demon is inside a person or just tormenting their thoughts, let's not be overly concerned about where the evil force is located and instead focus on how Jesus helps us achieve victory over it.

In addition to fervent prayer, repentance, and studying God's Word, believers must renounce any activities that expose them to demonic activity. This includes everything from unforgiveness and anger to idolatry, sexual immorality, and occult practices (Ephesians 4: 17–29; 5:13; Colossians 3:5). Our victory emanates from the indwelling of the Holy Spirit, but we cannot continue to live recklessly and expect that power to be the dominant force in our lives.

None of us can say with absolute certainty how the powers of evil operate in the life of a believer, but I find comfort in the fact that the solution is the same. It is putting our faith in Christ and pursuing a life of holiness alongside others who encourage and love us. It is meditating on God's Word, praying over ourselves and others, and repenting and renouncing sin that keeps us bound.

"Submit therefore to God. Resist the devil and he will flee from you."

—*James 4:7*

——— TWENTY-ONE ———

See Things in a New Way

We all have experienced dilemmas—difficulties we cannot initially figure out how to resolve. Sometimes, those dilemmas present as times of great uncertainty.

Here's the remarkable thing. If we can change our perspective—to see our lives in new and challenging ways—we can be guided by the extraordinary power of God in those times of difficulty.

To see how that works, think about the story of the Israelites at the Red Sea.

Victory seemed impossible, yet God specifically led them the long way around to demonstrate His astonishing miracle. It is one of recorded history's greatest demonstrations of God's power. Moses led the children of Israel through the Red Sea on dry ground, enabling them to escape the pursuing Egyptian army. When Pharaoh's army tried to follow, the massive walls of water came crashing down and drowning them. The children of Israel arrived safely at the other side.

What do we learn from Moses and the band of Israelites at the Red Sea?

We learn that it is never just about us. We are all here to advance the Kingdom of God, so it's always greater than just you or me. It is about His glory being made manifest on earth.

God may very well allow you to get into a situation that only *He* can get you out of. Sometimes, God will put you in a dilemma, and all He wants you to do is stand still. At other times, He may command you to move forward, even if you don't know the way. At those times, you move!

Faith often operates in the presence of fear. The children of Israel plunged ahead into the water of the Red Sea even though they were afraid. They followed their leader, Moses, who was in direct communication with God, who parted the waters so the people could cross on dry land.

Sometimes, God will even harden the hearts of others to push you in the direction He wants you to go. This is so beautiful because it's at the core of forgiveness. There is no need to hold grudges against people because, in reality, it was God's will for it to happen to you. When we're walking in God's way, He will inspire people to do things that inevitably work in our favor.

So, look at the dilemmas in your life in a new way. Be patient. Wait for God's power to come. If you know you are not living in accordance with the will of God, then start obeying the will of God so He can turn your situation around. Walk in faith. Relish the adventure of being God's loyal soldier.

When I became a follower of Christ, I came up against the whole Islamic world, which involved risking very real physical danger. Yet, I know it is not my battle. *It is the Lord's battle.* It's so much bigger than me. He gave me a purpose, and I'm walking according to that purpose. For that reason, I know He will protect me.

You, I, and all Christ followers do not fight this battle alone. We take up our positions. We stand firm and remain watchful for the deliverance the Lord will give us.

Do not be afraid. Do not be discouraged. Face whatever the Lord has given you—and know that the Lord will be with you.

22

─── TWENTY-TWO ───

Hearing from God During Difficult Times

"Peace I leave with you; my peace I give you. I do not give to you as the world gives. Do not let your hearts be troubled and do not be afraid."

—John 14:26–27

During difficult times, many of us may struggle with faith—faith in our political system, laws, the future, and even our rights and liberties in the United States. We are facing many changes, and combined, they seem to put us all at risk in a world that no longer looks very stable.

In times like this, Christians should maintain unwavering faith in the Lord and the indwelling of the Holy Spirit in every one of us. Faith is trusting in what God says until we see what God does. Acting on faith regarding even one word from God can change the course of our lives forever.

The one who accepts Jesus as their Lord is saved, but the relationship does not end there. Jesus left the Holy Spirit with us, so the relationship of rescuing, advising, and comforting us is an ongoing process. Our soul is saved in an instant, but the battlefield of our mind and heart endures. That's why it's so important to believe in the triune nature of God. God the Father is the Master of Creation, the Grand Architect who sets the plan and process in place. Jesus, God the Son, is how the divine plan of salvation is executed through His willingness to pay the price for our sins and through His act of rising again on the third day. God, the Holy Spirit, is how believers can consistently tap into that plan in a way that provides power and guidance for our lives.

Many of us struggle with hearing and obeying the word of God. As I explained, the notion that God would talk to me was initially hard to accept. As I was learning *how* to recognize His voice, I didn't always listen to what I heard; you might be able to relate to that. I experienced great disappointment and agony in those failures. Yet, the more I failed in doing it my way, the easier it got to follow His lead. Through prayer, reading the Word, and just spending quiet time contemplating God, things began to change. The Holy Spirit encouraged me, picked me up when I failed, and comforted me when I felt defeated. I wanted to punish myself, but He does not do that to us. He loves us into submission. It was almost like being a child again. Sometimes, we listen to our parents because we love and trust them. Other times, we just want to touch the hot stove. However, once burned, we learn.

As the world gets darker and bleaker, Christians need the wisdom from the Bible to become clearer and louder. This can happen only when we spend more time in worship, contemplation, fasting, and prayer. We each need to have a deep, personal relationship with the Holy Spirit. *We* don't know the future, but we can follow a God who does, both globally and for each one of us individually.

That's why there's so much opposition to the church and followers of Christ. If the word of God goes forth, things will change dramatically. We know that many forces are fighting against the change God could bring, but the best part is that God is independent. He does not rely on governments or anything or anyone else. The power of God's Word creates everything. He does it in the entire universe and will do it in your personal life.

Reading the Bible is essential, but there are additional resources that can help you begin a life-changing conversation with Christ. You've undoubtedly heard many negative things about social media, but it can be instrumental in your journey if used correctly. You can follow pastors whose messages are Biblically sound and resonate with you. Those channels will lead you to others who are in the same genre. It's an adventure, so have fun exploring! Just ensure those you follow are rooted in the Bible and preach that saving faith in Jesus is the only way to God.

Another way to begin your conversation with Christ is to worship as part of a church congregation. Today, many churches across the United States and abroad are non-denominational. Instead of focusing on a particular set of beliefs or customs, these churches cater to the modern understandings of believers who are specifically looking for a relationship with Christ. I describe them as *revival churches*—those that take the best of all the traditions to give their members all that Christ has to offer without limiting themselves to custom. As stated above, just make sure that whatever church you choose is firmly rooted in Biblical teachings and that the pastor embodies those teachings.

Suppose you have a physical or emotional barrier that prevents you from attending a local church. In that case, you might benefit from an online church family that will help you develop a personal relationship with Christ. The pastors of many online churches do everything from managing a live chat for online viewers to providing a host of virtual life groups to join based on your interests. They can also help you plan a visit whenever you are able to attend in person.

During difficult times, Christians must rely on what God speaks to move forward in faith. Those who have not accepted Christ may choose another object in which to have faith, but all of them lead to disappointment. Remember how Abraham held on to God's promises until he saw them manifest? We must hold on to God's promises until we see them come to pass.

This is no time to let up or to wander off the path. The worse it gets out there, the better it must be in the body of Christ. It is up to faith-filled Christians to give our friends, neighbors, and co-workers the hope and the joy of the Gospel of Jesus Christ.

It doesn't matter where we live or where we come from; the salvation of Jesus Christ is the solution for all of us.

TWENTY-THREE

The Diminishing Church

Sadly, the number of Christians in this country is dwindling—and even among those who still profess to be Christian, things have drastically changed.

Let's start by looking at the cold, hard numbers. In 1980, more than 90 percent of Americans said they were Christians. Today, it is less than 70 percent.

Okay, that means that about two-thirds of the people in America profess to be Christians. That's not *too* bad, you may think. Except, are those who profess Christianity *really* believers? Only *six percent* of those who say they are Christian have a Biblical worldview. Even more distressing, a large percentage of self-professed "Christians" do not believe the Holy Spirit is real or that the Bible is the inerrant Word of God. Many do not think faith in Jesus Christ is the only way to Heaven. Jesus is not central to their faith, *yet* they still call themselves Christians.

This dramatic decline in the core principles among American Christians corresponds to the rise of the millennials and non-Christian religions.

As the lead researcher of the study on Christians in America explains,

> "This new America we see emerging is radically different—demographically, politically, relationally and spiritually. It is a young, non-white, mobile population. This group is largely indifferent to the United States and is demonstrably skeptical of the nation's history, foundations, traditions, and ways of life. They are technologically advanced, sexually unrestrained, emotionally unpredictable, and a spiritual hybrid.[4]"

This new breed of Christians is also increasingly embracing the "woke culture" of hating American values and rewriting our history. Without the anchor of Biblical truths, people start to believe the lies that whites are inherently racist, gender is a choice, and all paths to God are equally good. We see this happening across the country in churches that supported the lawlessness during rampant looting and riots, and we see it in the churches that legitimize and perform same-sex marriages. Those caught up in such activities and attitudes:

> *"Perish because they refused to love the truth and so be saved. For this reason, God sends them a powerful delusion so that they will believe the lie."*
>
> —*2 Thessalonians 2:10–11*

---

[4] CRC_AWVI2021_Release04_Digital_01_20210608.pdf (arizonachristian.edu)

Delusions can damage all of us if we reject the truth of God's laws because they are uncomfortable or undesirable in today's culture. If we then act on a delusion, there can be severe and dangerous consequences. If we are unwilling to defend that Jesus is God incarnate and that He is the only means to eternal life, other principles take root and destroy the existing social structure. We are witnessing this across America and Europe.

As a counter-terrorism researcher and former Muslim, I can attest to how radical Islamic groups have undermined Western educational systems, the political landscape, and local community relations. Whether by birth rates, education, or violence, it has always been their stated goal to turn all of the West into Muslim nations. Therefore, it should not be surprising that the spiritual makeup of America is radically changing.

Dr. George Barna, director of research at the Cultural Research Center at Arizona Christian University, attributes this dramatic shift in beliefs to the fact that churches are ill-equipped to minister to the new demographic. He says churches need bold leadership that allows freedom to be creative while holding firm to Biblical principles. From my perspective, the future of American Christianity depends on how *fearlessly* the church will preach and defend Biblical truths.

I spent decades engrossed in the false religion of Islam, and I came to faith in Christ through the internet. I was drawn to the unequivocal promise of the Lord Jesus Christ that if I accepted the free gift of salvation, I would personally receive the power of God within me. I would no longer be praying to a distant and vengeful god but would have a supernatural relationship with a God who was still alive and performing miracles! It was a simple yet compelling fundamental truth about the God of the Bible. It testified to me that only *He* can do the impossible.

As the church debates holding on to the absolutes set forth by God Himself, how many of our young people are entranced by witchcraft and the occult? How many are joining New Age groups that promise healing and magical powers? I knew *thousands* of Christians who came to the cult of Islam also seeking power and strength. I myself endured layers of clothing in the sweltering heat and changed my entire way of life because I thought Islam had a mighty and awe-inspiring god. Then I learned how much mightier and more awe-inspiring is the Lord Jesus Christ!

As the Scripture testifies in the words of Jesus:

> *"Whoever believes in me will also do the works that I do; and greater works than these will he do, because I am going to the Father."*
>
> *—John 14:12*

Jesus healed the blind, raised the dead, and cast out demons with a single word—yet every believer can do even more. Receiving the Holy Spirit and having the righteousness of Christ within us is the transformative power to break addictions and change lives. Without Him, we are just another religion in an old book.

Jesus will return one day for His church, but do we have a sense of urgency in the meantime to protect His Bride (see Matthew 25:1–18)? In the book of Revelation, Jesus rebukes five out of seven churches to warn us that worldly desires and false teachings will corrupt people. His call to repentance teaches us how to survive the onslaught of deception and evil that fills the earth before His return. We also know from the study of End Times Scripture, like our opening verse, that this apostasy in the church does not surprise God. In fact, we are right on schedule.

My husband was a Christian for 20 years before he heard anything about the End Times. It is astounding how many times I have since heard that exact sentiment. Though an essential part of the Christian faith, *eschatology*—the study of theology involved with death, judgment, and the final destiny of the soul and humankind—is largely avoided or ignored because many churches don't take the Bible literally or are afraid of causing dissension.

Unfortunately, churches today take tremendous liberties with what they teach as the fundamentals of the Christian faith. They seem to take those liberties because they fear offending members who may then leave their congregations if they find the truth to be too hard. In my opinion, preserving authentic Christianity will not happen by having more pastors in skinny jeans preaching false or creative interpretations of Scripture. I am fortunate to be under the discipleship of an authentic Bible teacher, Pastor Jack Hibbs of Calvary Chapel Chino Hills. He provides the unadulterated teaching of the whole counsel of God. This includes the promises of peace, ease during suffering, and the eventual fall of humanity into depravity. Many will be called, but few will be chosen to withstand it.

The Apostle Paul said it plainly:

> *"My speech and my preaching was not with enticing words of man's wisdom, but in demonstration of the Spirit and of power: That your faith should not stand in the wisdom of men, but in the power of God."*

> *—1 Corinthians 2:4–5*

TWENTY-FOUR

Who Are the Extremists?

As Christians, it is our responsibility to defend our Biblical values. However, with all the upheaval that is becoming the norm in this nation, how do we stand for our principles when it's likely that Christians are going to be the target of radical persecution?

Many signs have pointed to that kind of oppression, and unfortunately, it seems that time is here.

In my work as a United States government contractor, I helped build community-based programs that would detect and deter Islamic radicals. We used words like *violent extremists* instead of *Islamic* to distinguish between peaceful Muslims and those who used religion to justify violence. The fundamental U.S. policy was that *words matter*—we took pride in protecting religious liberty and the freedom to express unpopular beliefs.

Recently, however, many of our elected officials have been unwilling to apply those same principles to conservatives and Christians — the right to freely express their political or religious beliefs, however unpopular it may be in today's debased culture.

The aftermath of the January 6, 2021, attack on the United States Capitol is an important example of what happens when you demonize an entire segment of mainstream society. Though a relatively tiny group of people were involved in the violence, the entire conservative movement was described as one of violent radicals who must be identified, marginalized, and even subjected to criminal penalties. Many who entered the Capitol peacefully remained incarcerated for years without being charged with a crime. They were held in jail cells not necessarily for their actions but for their beliefs. Some pleaded guilty to crimes they didn't commit so they could go home to their families. For many, their only actual "crime" was expressing their constitutional rights to freedom of speech and assembly.

The January 6 incident is only one example of the kind of persecution that is occurring. It is incredibly alarming to hear Congressional representatives talk about their fellow Americans with disdain and intolerance. It was horrible to hear former President Biden refer to the nearly 75 million people who voted for Trump as "MAGA extremists." Millions of Americans are vilified because they passionately defend the rights of the unborn, adhere to and defend Biblical gender roles, and stand by the Christian ideals that are the cornerstone of our Constitution.

This kind of vilification can and will have dangerous and far-reaching consequences.

Conservative Christians are not inherently violent or intolerant. Islamic terrorists explicitly advocate violence in seeking to establish their society, but Christians do not seek to impose their values through violence. Yet some in the media and government equate Christians with Islamic terrorists as if Christians are the new "enemy of the state."

How will Christian leaders respond to that kind of gross mischaracterization? For that matter, how will members of the church at large respond? Do we have the internal fortitude and courage to defend our ideals even if we become social outcasts or suffer physical consequences?

In the book of Revelation, God tells us that the devil will put some in prison to test us and that some will suffer persecution. He also promises that if we are faithful, even to the point of death, He will give us a victor's crown. He teaches us that we must be bold during such times, whatever the cost, and never fear the consequences that men can bring.

The Apostle Paul knew this principle all too well. He experienced physical torture, imprisonment, and ridicule. He refused to denounce His belief in Christ even to the point of death. Why? He had an unwavering devotion to preaching the Gospel.

Salvation occurs at the moment we accept Jesus Christ as our Lord and Savior, but that is not the only goal of our redemption. We are called to preach the Gospel so that the whole world can be redeemed and placed perfectly whole at the throne of God. The fact that we get to experience sanctification and the joy that comes from a relationship with Christ is a welcomed byproduct, but it is not the primary objective. We cannot forget that the Great Commission (see Matthew 28: 19-20) is to reconcile the whole world unto Him, *regardless of the personal cost.*

We all need the grace and peace that can come only from a relationship with Jesus Christ. Now more than ever, our society needs Christians to provide a way out of the turmoil of personal circumstances.

The power of redemption does *not* rely on who occupies the White House or what society says is acceptable. Instead, it is based on God's infallible Word found in the Bible as it goes forth from the church. The Bible and the truths it contains are the only unwavering source of peace in what would otherwise be a chaotic world.

Embrace your Christianity and continue to nurture your relationship with the Savior of all humanity. Regardless of others' efforts to characterize us as extremists or radicals, we know the true power of Jesus Christ to redeem, restore, and transform the lives of all who accept Him.

Never forget:

"For God so loved the world, that He gave His only Son, so that everyone who believes in Him will not perish but have eternal life."

—John 3:16

As you continue to preach and live as He prescribes, stay focused not on the fear of persecution but on the promise of eternal life—a promise from the one who never breaks His promises.

TWENTY-FIVE

Introducing the Gospel
to Muslims

As followers of Christ, we have the profound honor of sharing the Gospel with others. Since I lived more than two decades as a Muslim, I am often asked what is the best way to introduce Muslims to God's Word.

Whether it is to family members, friends, or new acquaintances—there are many different opinions on how to introduce Christianity to Muslims. Some say it's best to simply live your life as an example of a "good Christian." Others feel that apologetics is the best approach to defending or proving the truth of Christian principles.

Though most Christians' natural inclination in approaching Muslims is apologetics, it often turns into arguments about doctrine and hurling insults about Islam that alienate the listener. I believe the real power lies in the reality of the Trinity—God the Loving Father, His only begotten Son Jesus Christ, and the indwelling of the Holy Spirit.

As you introduce Muslims to Christianity, be very clear that the Trinity is three manifestations of the one true God and not three separate gods. We have God the Father who loves us; He came down in the form of His Son to save us, and He leaves us His Holy Spirit to guide us. Muslims accuse Christians of being polytheists because they do not understand this. Unfortunately, many Christians cannot properly articulate it, so it is critical that you understand and explain it clearly to any Muslim who is investigating Christianity.

Having left Islam, it saddens me to hear even Christians make the false claim that we all worship the same God and that each religious path can lead to the "truth." Do not be content to give false or comfortable versions of a "truth" that leaves the individual without salvation and the love of God that comes through faith in Christ.

> *Jesus answered, "I am the way and the truth and the life. No one comes to the Father except through me."*
>
> *—John 14:6*

The person you speak to may not readily accept what you are saying, but that is not your concern. There is only one God, and no one will reach His presence except through faith in Christ. I understand and believe that now, but I did not think that as a Muslim. Very few do. I wish someone had the courage to say it to me earlier.

Finally, I always end any discussion with a Muslim by challenging them to pray for God to reveal Himself and the reality of Jesus Christ. A Muslim's mind may fight the truth of what you have said, but trust in God's power to lead them to the truth.

If you live in an area with many Muslim refugees, consider hosting an open house, either in a home or local church. Invite the new refugees for a meal and a presentation on the basics of life in America. We are a predominantly Christian nation, so it's perfectly reasonable to explain the fundamentals of Christianity in that presentation. Allow the participants to share their faith as well. Do not be afraid to have a dialogue about our different beliefs.

To be clear, I am not suggesting an interfaith event where we seek to find commonalities between Islam and Christianity worshipping one God—quite the opposite. The ultimate goal is to highlight the differences—how belief in the Lord Jesus Christ guarantees forgiveness of sins, eternal life, and the indwelling of the Holy Spirit, who provides a personal relationship with God.

Focus on the truth of our beliefs and let the Lord do the rest.

The presenter at such a meeting does not have to be a pastor but should be knowledgeable enough to articulate the fundamentals of salvation and the Trinity if challenged. Remember, one of the biggest hurdles for Muslims is the notion that Christians worship multiple gods. Therefore, as mentioned, we must emphasize that we worship one God manifested in three persons, not three separate gods.

Once you have chosen a location and a presenter for your gathering, it is vital to designate a translator! Since many refugees work with Americans in their home countries, finding someone who can interpret for the rest should not be difficult. The one who translates often gets an extra blessing; I have a dear friend who came to faith by being a translator for a local church. It is an excellent opportunity for that individual to have the power of the Gospel flow directly through them.

Remember, too, that you should serve culturally sensitive food. Muslims do not eat pork, and most do not drink alcohol, so avoiding those items would be a welcomed sign of respect.

Whenever you worry about witnessing to a Muslim, remember the story of Ananias. He heard the voice of the Lord telling him to go and speak with Saul, who was a notoriously vicious and evil man, persecuting the believers. Saul had experienced a mighty change of heart and later became Paul, who served as a powerful preacher—but Ananias feared him as a man who had done great harm to the saints in Jerusalem. (see Acts 9:10–19). In response to Ananias's fear, the Lord said, *"Go! This man is my chosen instrument to proclaim my name."*

What do we take from that encounter? We never know who the Lord has predestined to receive salvation. We cannot know who will become a Spirit-filled believer, but He does. I consider myself one of the most unlikely believers and yet here I am writing this book! God is so great; never underestimate who He will call to Himself.

I pray that watching the heart-wrenching tragedy of Christians persecuted in Muslim lands does not harden our hearts toward these new immigrants. Many have fled the brutality of the dictators, hoping for a better life here in America. Instead of reacting with hardened hearts, let us unite in prayer, asking the Lord that for every Christian who is harmed, thousands of Muslims will become soldiers of Christ.

TWENTY-SIX

Beware of the Wolves in Sheep's Clothing

"Beware of false prophets, who come to you in sheep's clothing, but inwardly they are ravenous wolves."

—*Matthew 7:15*

Wouldn't it be wonderful if every Christian leader was righteous and pure in representing Jesus Christ?

I have to believe that most of them are, but sadly, we know that some of them are not. It is essential to learn and discern the difference between the two. Their potential for doing damage is great, particularly when it comes to permitting sexual immorality.

The Lord gave us a stern warning:

"Beware of false prophets, who come to you in sheep's clothing, but inwardly they are ravenous wolves."

—*Matthew 7:15*

Beware—in other words, being aware— means the onus is on us to safeguard the community against people who could do harm with false doctrine or who indulge in immoral behavior. To safeguard others, we must be alert.

Whether it is outright misstatements of God's Word or actions that implicitly condone unbiblical behavior, allowing such conduct to go unchecked can have far-reaching consequences. It damages the reputation of Christians as a whole and causes irreparable harm to the many who suffer at the hands of these individuals.

Consider the utmost importance God places on the sanctity of the marriage covenant. As a former Muslim, I can attest to the rampant abuse that Muslim women endure—the worst of which is being forced into illegal, polygamous relationships. In those situations, neither the women nor the children have any legal rights and are subject to constant mistreatment and ridicule in the community. Though many Muslim men do not engage in polygamy, the practice is permissible under Islamic law. That air of legitimacy causes the most harm because it gives the man a religious justification to force a woman's acceptance of polygamy. I know this sorrow firsthand. I naively assumed that I had no right to deny it since god allowed it.

For me and other former Muslim women, one of the most appealing aspects of Christianity is that God commands monogamy. A husband and wife become one flesh (see Mark 10:6–9) and have a responsibility to honor and love one another (see Ephesians 5:3–6). Adultery and other forms of sexual depravity are repeatedly condemned throughout the Bible.

The Apostle Paul explicitly warns believers that God's wrath will come on the "sons of disobedience" who engage in sexual sin (see Ephesians 5:3–6). Jesus said that even lusting after a woman was committing adultery in the heart (see Matthew 5:28). With such stern warnings, how can we allow such behavior to go unchecked, especially among our leaders and teachers?

In one celebrated example, many well-known Christian pastors and leaders have come out strongly against the despicable abuse committed by the late Ravi Zacharias. He purportedly engaged in acts of rape, unwanted touching of numerous women, and spiritual abuse.

Though he was first accused in 2017 of unwanted sexual advances, Zacharias's conduct went unchallenged and was revealed only when he died.

In another egregious example of sexual misconduct, former Hillsong Church Pastor Carl Lentz was fired for "leadership issues and moral failures" after one of several extramarital affairs became public. Though Lentz has been removed from his leadership position at Hillsong, this is another case where action was not taken in anywhere close to a timely manner. A staff member reported Lentz's inappropriate conduct as far back as 2017, but it was vehemently denied.

In both these examples, action was taken only once the behavior became publicly undeniable and many lives were irreparably harmed. As Southern Baptist leader Russell Moore so aptly put it, "This awful report—coming on the heels of so many other situations detailed before—should rouse the conscience to ask not just how sadists can get into places of Christian leadership, but whether we have created a situation where the very presence of a conscience is an impediment to advancement in . . . some sectors of American Christianity."

The pastors and leaders who have come out against such behavior encourage not only the repentance of any leaders still engaging in illicit sexual behavior; they also advocate for accountability of all church leaders who are in a position to manipulate the spiritual and emotional needs of their members.

Simply having someone caught apologize and wish them well in their future endeavors does not solve the problem. It does not create a sense of accountability. That approach is offensive to the rest of us, who endure the ridicule of outsiders accusing "the church" of hypocrisy and corruption. Church members, elders, and leaders must demand stricter policies for investigating claims of misconduct if they want to demonstrate their commitment to the Gospel of Jesus Christ.

The Gospel firmly teaches accountability and holiness. The Scriptures tell us that we must be holy because He is holy (see 1 Peter 1:16). The Church is one body, and when one part is hurting, we all suffer.

We all are responsible for living a life that honors one another and the Holy Spirit that dwells within us. Though we all fall short sometimes, the Lord holds our leaders to an even higher standard, and the church should do the same. Final judgment is for God alone, but that is not an excuse to let evil actions run rampant.

Suppose we fail to hold fast to the sacred tenets that set us apart as followers of Christ. In that case, we risk becoming the exact type of people that Christ warned us about:

> *"Many will say to me on that day, Lord, Lord, did we not prophesy in your name and in your name drive out demons and, in your name, perform many miracles? Then I will tell them plainly, I never knew you. Away from me, you evildoers!"*
>
> *—Matthew 7:22*

TWENTY-SEVEN

The Celebrity Pastor Paradox

"You need milk, not solid food, for everyone who lives on milk is unskilled in the word of righteousness since he is a child. But solid food is for the mature, for those who have their powers of discernment trained by constant practice to distinguish good from evil."

—Hebrews 5:12–14

Much criticism is directed at megachurch pastors, claiming they preach what they do not emulate. Many of them engage in extravagant lifestyles with expensive wardrobes and jet-setting around the world for exotic vacations. More troublesome for people like me is their failure to teach the whole counsel of God. Their obsession with social media fame, personal popularity, and wealth accumulation leads to intentionally omitting the hard truths of Christ's message. Constant themes in the Bible include the need to repent and turn from sin, to avoid conforming to patterns of this world, and to be willing to face persecution for our beliefs. When these truths are absent, a church body becomes more like a self-help group or a social club than a place of discipleship.

I am eternally grateful that the Lord led me to find a Bible-based pastor to grow in the knowledge of righteousness. However, I cannot dismiss that I was drawn to Christ and fed the milk of the Gospel through a celebrity pastor.

I witnessed hundreds of new believers come through the megachurch I belonged to. Though I do not know how many became true believers, I remember the parable of the wheat and the tares. The Lord teaches that it is not for us as servants to uproot what the enemy sows because we may lose the good in the process. (see Matthew 13:24-30)

As a community of believers, we must do everything in our power to prevent corruption in the church. Using the standards of corporate America rather than Christ will only lead to further moral decay. We are also commanded to guard against false teachers and those that come as wolves in sheep's clothing to mislead the flock (see Matthew 7:15). Finally, our church attendance should be focused on drawing near to God, not idolizing a preacher and his hip sense of style.

All this being true, we cannot dismiss how God uses some of these institutions to draw in people like me. Maybe I would have eventually found my way to Christ through another means, but the wisdom of the parable gives me pause. He says:

> *"Let both grow together until the harvest, and at the time of harvest, I will say to the reapers, First gather together the tares and bind them in bundles to burn them, but gather the wheat into my barn."*
>
> —*Matthew 13:30*

TWENTY-EIGHT

Deconstructing Christianity

"Whoever acknowledges me before others, I will also acknowledge before my Father in Heaven. But whoever disowns me before others, I will disown before my Father in Heaven."

—Matthew 10:32–33

Is it possible for a dedicated Christ follower to lose faith and wander off the path? I wonder. Someone determined to find an error with God will find justification to deny His word and His plan for our lives.

One famous example is Barry "Phanatik" Goodwin, co-founder of the Cross Movement. His fans loved him as a great lyricist, a committed Christian, and a stalwart preacher of the Gospel. Then things changed for him. He provides an example of why it is so important to avoid attaching ourselves to a single Christ follower.

In a personal and heartfelt video, Phanatik told his fans that there were "issues" in the Scripture he could no longer ignore. His conscience no longer allowed him to continue to preach and believe in the Gospel. He did not articulate the specific issues he had with Christianity. The only specific example he provided was that his crisis of faith began in 2014, a time when he also started suffering from depression.

Phanatik was not a self-taught Christian like I am. He spent years studying Scripture in Bible college and also attended Westminster Seminary. Toward the end of the video, he clarifies his intention to publicly state his problems with the Bible, so I presume a lengthy intellectual debate eventually ensued. I will leave that discussion for scholars far more capable than I am. Instead, I want to focus on the tragedy of someone walking away from Jesus.

I do not know how Phanatik first encountered the Lord, but as I've already described, I met Him at the darkest point in my life.

We were all sinners who need a Savior. God loves us, but He is holy. He could not ignore the price of sin, so He sent His Son to pay that price on our behalf. The Apostle Paul explained in glorious plainness that redemption requires us to accept what Jesus did for us on the cross:

> *"God presented Christ as a sacrifice of atonement, through the shedding of His blood—to be received by faith. He did this to demonstrate His righteousness, because in His forbearance, He had left the sins committed beforehand unpunished— He did it to demonstrate His righteousness at present, so as to be just and the one who justifies those who have faith in Jesus."*
>
> *—Romans 3:25-26*

I am eternally grateful the Lord did not leave me blind to the essential and straightforward reality that my salvation depends on faith in Christ—faith that is:

> *"The substance of things hoped for, the evidence of things not seen."*
>
> *—Hebrews 11:1*

There is overwhelming historical evidence that Jesus walked the earth, and His arrival fulfilled nearly 300 prophecies written more than 700 years beforehand. Even with that evidence, we must personally have faith. We need faith in what we cannot see.

I wonder how many nights Phanatik spent on his knees crying to God, seeking His face, and praying for the answers to his unbelief. We know he sought out scholars, both liberal and conservative. Did he turn to God, the author and finisher of our faith?

Some commentators opine that Phanatik's departure from Christianity resulted from "church hurt." Whether it's a perceived lack of social justice in the evangelical community or individuals who disappointed him, we cannot judge Christ by what people do. We are all wretched sinners saved by grace. We make mistakes and commit offenses knowingly and unknowingly. Some of us try diligently to avoid it, but others do not. None of our shortcomings or lack of moral clarity should detract from the purity and grace of Christ. It is a relationship, not religion, that saves us. When the trials of life, like depression or disappointment from family or church friends, strike us at our core, our strength comes from the great consoler who helps us hold on and persevere. The Bible warns us repeatedly about relying on our emotions to govern our faith because the heart is deceptively wicked. I can understand the agony and frustration that would make someone want to leave a church, but I cannot understand walking away from Jesus.

I know what it is like to wander around without a relationship with Jesus Christ. It's something I would not wish on my worst enemy. However, the Lord expects our reverence and awe to transcend our curious minds. I cannot pretend to know the struggles Phanatik had when he engaged the Scriptures, but I genuinely pray he and others find their way back.

PART 4

THE CULTURE WAR

"This is war, and there is no neutral ground. If you're not on my side, you're the enemy; if you're not helping, you're making things worse."

—*Luke 11:23*

TWENTY-NINE

The Parental Rights Movement

"We are from God, and whoever knows God listens to us; but whoever is not from God does not listen to us. This is how we recognize the Spirit of truth and the spirit of falsehood."

—1 John 4:6

It has become increasingly apparent that our families and our children are under attack in this nation. Our ability to protect our families—the foundation of our civilization—is becoming ever more critical.

Let's look at some of the things that are happening.

Anarchy broke out at a school board meeting in New Jersey when a group of disgruntled and courageous parents protested the decision to rename Columbus Day to Indigenous People's Day. Sadly, though, the name Columbus Day was eliminated. Instead of reinstating the holiday's name, the *Wall Street Journal* reported that the board made the ridiculous decision to cancel the names of *all* the national holidays and instead call them "days off."

If you don't see a problem with that, consider this: that battle is further evidence of the alarming trend to indoctrinate the hearts and minds of our children with the idea that the foundations of American society are inherently oppressive, racist, and sexist.

This wave started back in 2019 with the fierce debate about including same-sex relationships when teaching "health" education in our schools. Despite protests from parents, the California Board of Education approved the use of new textbooks and classroom discussions that included nonbinary explanations of gender and same-sex relationships. As a result, regardless of a family's personal religious and moral beliefs, middle-school children across America are now taught that there are more than two genders—and that, in fact, those genders can be changed at will. They are also taught that same-sex relationships are a perfectly normal alternative to traditional male and female roles.

In 2020, we saw violent uprisings to remove statues and rename schools whose names were considered offensive because they supposedly glorify a racist and painful past. Historian Julian Hayter of the University of Richmond claimed that "for this country to move beyond its tortured racial history, we must deal with the symbols of oppression. We must deal with the symbols of white supremacy."[5]

The battle continues to rage over the imposition of Critical Race Theory (CRT) in schools. This doctrine provides the justification for all these individual attempts to remake our society from the ground up, and it starts with our children.

People in positions of power throughout academia, the media, and local government are buying into the notion that "truth" is a matter of perspective. A byproduct of "wokeism" gaining prominence in our society is the idea that all applications of truth are actually applications of power that can and should be changed. In other words, the truth is based on power and who drives the narrative. *The* truth is replaced with *my* truth.

---

[5] https://www.businessinsider.com/confederate-statues-removal-slavery-protests-2020-6?op=1

When "truth" becomes subjective, how can a society uphold any semblance of law and order? Whose moral standards do we use to decide when life begins, how we define marriage or gender, and the correct path to achieving racial equality?

Islamic law explicitly allows its adherents to deceive others by not practicing the faith in times of war or conflict so they can gain a political or physical advantage. I believe that is why American Muslim congresswomen and many Muslim activists support the radical left agenda—even though it is antithetical to the religious tenets of Islam on issues of gender, marriage, abortion, and racial equality. They do so because weakening the Judeo-Christian foundation of the country serves the cause of Islam.

However, followers of Christ know that deception is *not* a prescription against worldly trouble. In the Bible, which is God's eternal truth and guide for humanity, all these questions have an answer, and those answers are immutable. They are not up for interpretation or subject to change. We cannot compromise these principles we are called to defend and uphold.

God knew that these kinds of battles would arise, and He forewarned us of that fact. He also gave us a clear description of how to defend ourselves, holding fast to the truth:

> *"Therefore, put on the full armor of God, so that when the day of evil comes, you may be able to stand your ground, and after you have done everything, to stand. Stand firm then, with the belt of truth buckled around your waist, with the breastplate of righteousness in place, and with your feet fitted with the readiness that comes from the Gospel of peace."*
>
> *—Ephesians 6:13–15*

Despite the turmoil and upheaval we see around us, Christians should have unwavering certainty in answering all these questions. We are called to be set apart. We do not conform to the patterns of this world (see Romans 12:2). As a royal priesthood, we cannot succumb to political or social pressure to redefine God's truth.

Instead, we proclaim His excellencies so others may be called out of darkness into His marvelous light (see 1 Peter 2:9).

In so doing, we protect the children and families of this nation.

THIRTY

Defeating the LGBTQ Messaging Aimed at Our Kids

"Or do you not know that the unrighteous will not inherit the Kingdom of God? Do not be deceived: neither the sexually immoral, nor idolaters, nor adulterers, nor men who practice homosexuality, nor thieves, nor the greedy, nor drunkards, nor revilers, nor swindlers will inherit the Kingdom of God."

—1 Corinthians 6:9-10

The fight to protect the values our children are exposed to has reached a significant turning point, as evidenced by the strong reactions to Disney's recent policies and programming decisions. To encourage acceptance of the LGBTQ lifestyle, Disney senior executives have committed to integrating "queerness" into children's programming wherever possible. Karey Burke, a parent of gender dysphoric children, has echoed this commitment by promising to enhance LGBT representation in Disney's shows. Moreover, some of their staff reported changes in their interactions with children, as they are now instructed to avoid addressing them as "boys and girls." Gender-specific bathroom signs have also been replaced with neutral stick figures. Amplifying their stance, CEO Bob

Chapek has pledged to significantly boost Disney's funding for LGBT advocacy initiatives.

Though much of this battle has come to light since Disney was pressured to oppose the Florida parental rights bill, Disney's transformation has been going on for a long time. For years, Christian parents have been navigating the corrupt and collapsed culture of a once family-friendly brand. The movies consistently elevate central female characters who dare to reject tradition and exert their independence from conventional society. The programming blatantly rejects a Christian worldview of the family and God's view of human sexuality.

Fortunately, the parental rights movement sweeping the country refuses to remain silent any longer. Christian Post contributor Jerry Bower said it best: "Outrage is not enough. It's time for Christians to stop merely talking about Disney and start talking to them." There are several ways we can do that.

One of the most impactful ways is withdrawing our financial support for the Disney brand. That includes canceling Disney+ subscriptions and annual theme park passes and divesting from Disney stock. We must publicly express our disapproval with rallies, protests, and social media campaigns. Several Southern California churches and worship leaders have led the charge. Pastor Rob McCoy teamed up with prominent Christian activist Sean Ferucht, calling on the church to be bold and outspoken in defense of our children. Christian social media influencers have also taken to Instagram and Facebook to encourage public disappointment with Disney's stance.

Absent a sudden worldwide revival, we may never turn back the tide of an increasingly debased culture. However, we defend biblical values because that is what we are called to do as Christians, regardless of the personal consequences. Even the threat of death could not deter Peter and John from preaching what they knew.

> *"Do you think God wants us to obey you rather than Him? We cannot stop telling about everything we have seen and heard."*
>
> —*Acts 4: 19–20*

We also appreciate the suffering because:

"Suffering produces perseverance; perseverance, character."

—Romans 5: 3–4

Being a Christian today takes courage because everyone seems to be moving in the opposite direction.

So, the next time you pass your child on the couch watching a Disney show about same-sex parents and homosexual teenage romance, remember those messages will be imprinted in their minds and later reinforced by their peers. We must do everything we can to challenge this narrative because every child matters. The longer we stay silent, the worse it will get.

As society fights over gender identity and the treatment of same-sex relationships under the law, the church and we as parents need to address these issues head-on, even at the dinner table. If you are like me, these questions are a constant source of debate with teenage children who are bombarded with social media and classroom discussions that challenge our Biblical views on sexuality, marriage, and gender.

Alarming statistics from a recent Gallup poll show that the onslaught of LGBTQ+ messaging directed at our youth is working. The report states, "Younger generations are far more likely to consider themselves to be something other than heterosexual. This includes about one in six adult members of Generation Z (those aged 18 to 23 in 2020) . . . and more than half of those claim they are bisexual."[6] The fact that the rise is most pronounced in young people indicates that the deliberate indoctrination of our children *not* to accept traditional gender roles is increasingly successful.

When it comes to gender identity, the drastic rise in young people who identify as "gender fluid" has generated fierce debate. Prominent academics and health professionals advocate for a gender-affirmative

---

[6] https://news.gallup.com/poll/329708/lgbt-identification-rises-latest-estimate.aspx

model, claiming that gender is somehow determined by a combination of biology, development, and socialization, along with culture and context. Together, these factors whimsically create a person's gender. Therefore, this warped logic means that parents should accept the "gender" of a child as the child describes it, regardless of the child's anatomy.

Child advocates, researchers, and many Christians firmly believe the rapid onset of gender confusion in our youth results from underlying emotional disorders and manipulation from schools and other institutions that are engaged in some form of conversion therapy on our children. If you are not familiar with this debate, I encourage you to read as many resources as you can, including those referenced in this book, to understand the extent of the battle for our youths' identity and emotional well-being.

Surprisingly, the church as a whole is not of one opinion on the issue of sexual preference and God's condemnation of same-sex relations. On one side, the acceptance of openly gay members and clergy is on the rise. Some denominations that ordain homosexual pastors and worship leaders defend their stance by claiming Jesus loves everyone, and research shows that a significant number of Christians find no conflict between their religious beliefs and homosexuality.

Thankfully, there is another side that has very different opinions. Many evangelical pastors do not legitimize same-sex couples and instead encourage the individual to rebuke the sin and lean on the power of the Holy Spirit to fight the urges of same-sex attraction, just as one would do when addressing other sins like fornication or adultery. The movie *In His Image* does a beautiful job describing just how a Bible-honoring Christian can convey the love of Christ to someone struggling with same-sex attraction. Organizations like Changed Movement[7] help people find community with others who are struggling with similar issues but who left the LGBTQ+ lifestyle for freedom in Christ.

---

[7] https://changedmovement.com/

Even as a new believer, I knew the Lord did not intend to condone same-sex relationships based on Scripture, but I struggled with how I could convey these principles to my daughter in a spirit of love and compassion. I was fortunate to attend an event for Living Stone Ministries[8] at my church, where I heard from other parents of children struggling with gender identity and same-sex attraction.

It was a wonderful time of support and worship with other parents. Still, the most amazing part of the evening was listening to formerly gay believers talk about their journey and the impact their parents had on their road to freedom in Christ. Two of these young men and women emphatically said their parents' unwavering commitment to the Gospel stuck with them the most when they decided to leave the homosexual lifestyle. As one young man put it, "No matter how I tried to manipulate my mom or convince her that she was wrong and just didn't want to support me, she never wavered on the truth that Jesus wanted a better life for me, and I would never find true happiness in a same-sex relationship." The truth of his mother's words rang in his ears when he survived an attempted suicide and finally gave his life to Christ for healing and restoration.

Another young woman said her Christian mother took the opposite approach and went to gay bars with her to make her feel accepted. It ultimately backfired and made her resent her mother for not helping her leave the lifestyle.

Hearing these stories brought me so much peace because it was a truth I knew in my heart. Hearing it from someone who lived it affirmed my conviction.

So, despite the arguments and accusations that my stance is homophobic, outdated, or just "my truth," I continue to tell my young daughter that Jesus loves all sinners but despises the sin. It is no different than if she came to me wanting to do drugs or engage in premarital sex. I would warn her that a life of sin will never bring happiness or the freedom that comes from a life in obedience to God.

---

[8] https://www.livingstonesministries.org/

In light of all that is being thrown at our children to draw them into a life of death and depression, it is unfortunate that any church would condone same-sex couples and even allow openly gay pastors to lead a congregation. How can we teach our young people to follow any of the Bible's commandments if we compromise the one that destroys the sanctity of creation and monogamy between a man and a woman in marriage? It is just one more example of how liberalism is unraveling the fundamental principles of the Gospel.

Ultimately, it is a massive disservice to people who want to break the strongholds of addiction and be restored through the love and redemption of Christ.

THIRTY-ONE

The Skyrocketing Risk of Suicide

"The steadfast love of the Lord never ceases; His mercies never come to an end; they are new every morning; great is your faithfulness."

—Lamentations 3:22–23

Evil has come to take the minds of our children, confuse their God-given sexual identity, destroy families, and rewrite our history. If all of it is successful, then the only way out of that life of misery is suicide. The Surgeon General recently reported that our teenagers are more at risk of suicide than ever before in our nation's history. Their feelings of isolation, uncertainties about the future, substance abuse, and other forms of abuse occurring in the home have triggered soaring rates of depression, anxiety, and suicidal thoughts nationwide. Young people across every socioeconomic class, race, and ethnicity are affected, with 6,600 teenagers committing suicide in 2020 alone. Our children are dealing with more uncertainty than any other generation in history. The average

American youth will have seen close to 200,000 violent acts on some form of media by the time they turn eighteen, and most no longer live in two-parent households that provide emotional support. Consequently, many have an over-dependence on their peers, which ends up creating greater emotional instability.

In numerous studies, researchers have shown how the steady stream of violence from movies, television, and video games profoundly affects young minds. These media sources glorify aggression and numb children to the finality of death. The portrayal of heroes dying in romanticized manners often gives a false impression that death is somehow alluring.

The breakdown of the family unit also has played a significant role in increased suicide risk. In my generation, teens were surrounded by family, teachers, coaches, church youth groups, and other youth programs to keep us busy. Most of us had at least one best friend with several close friends. I often asked my daughter, "Don't you have a ride-or-die kind of friend?" Sadly, the answer is no. Many of our children are disconnected from nurturing peer relationships that are built on love, trust, and forgiveness. This used to be the normal American life for a young person. Today, many young people also lack the affection, provision, protection, and counsel of two parents. Instead of bonding with family members, they bond with fellow teens or strangers online. When unreliable friendships that can crumble for any reason are their foundation, our teens crumble with them.

Other prevailing factors include significant losses of loved ones or financial insecurity. People may also develop a fascination with the dark world as portrayed in popular television shows, movies, and video games. Additionally, the media can fuel a belief in imaginary friends whom they can converse with—friends who might encourage them to "end it all."

During a recent podcast episode, my husband and I were surprised to learn how many people in the church had been—and continue to be—affected by the horrible tragedy of suicide. Out of a dozen live listeners, five had an immediate family member who either attempted or committed suicide—including me.

In his early twenties, my husband had lost the will to live. He placed a loaded gun inside his mouth, determined to pull the trigger. The television was on in the background, and interestingly, a commercial about starving kids in Africa ultimately shocked him back into the reality that his life was worth living.

A woman in the podcast audience related that her son's girlfriend committed suicide right before Christmas; she was pregnant with his child. It shook the family to their core, but their faith in God is helping them heal.

I am not immune; I deal with the powerlessness that comes from being the parent of a child who struggles with mental illness and thoughts of suicide. My faith in the Lord Jesus Christ and knowing my daughter also has accepted Christ comforts me and allows me to surrender the burden to Him. Yet, I can't help but face the genuine notion that God is ultimately in control, and He is the only one who knows what life may have in store for any of us.

Kay Warren, a prominent Christian author and speaker whose son took his own life in 2013, eloquently expressed the paradox in this way: "My hope was pretty much centered around what could happen here. Rather than taking the longer view, sometimes things don't happen the way we want them to here on earth. Yet I can be safe and secure and even joyful with that confidence of what God is doing, ultimately."[9]

When anxiety about ourselves or our loved ones builds up inside, the real danger occurs when we turn away from the Lord and toward ourselves. Whether it's money, social distancing, escapism through substances, or other forms of abuse, anger, or resentment—none of these offers a real solution to the problem. In the midst of being threatened in any way, including the threat of possible suicide, we must realize God is our refuge. The pressures of life should lead us to run toward God for rest in His peace rather than running away from Him.

---

[9] https://www.christianpost.com/news/kay-warren-says-suicide-doesnt-condemn-believers-to-hell-says-she-prayed-audacious-prayers-before-son-took-his-life.html?page=2

Three truths can help each of us regain the perspective we need in times of darkness.

First, even if you are convinced that nobody else loves you, you must know that God does. He loves you with a love so profound that it is incomprehensible to us as mortals. In His own words, Jesus Himself said:

> *"For God so loved the world that He gave His one and only Son, that whoever believes in Him shall not perish but have eternal life."*
>
> *—John 3:16*

Second, the harsh reality is that if you choose to end your life, you end all your options and possibilities. Right now, while you still have air in your lungs, you have the possibility of hope, forgiveness, and redemption—no matter what you've done or what has been done to you.

The third simple truth is that it's not your life to take. The Scripture tells us:

> *"Know that the Lord is God. It is He who made us, and we are His; we are His people, the sheep of His pasture."*
>
> *—Psalm 100:3*

We do not belong to ourselves; God creates us. Each person is crafted with a specific purpose. Even if it doesn't seem apparent at the moment, life is a gift given by Him so that we can accomplish our mission on earth. Walking with the Lord and uncovering that purpose is the grand adventure we embark upon.

We all face very real threats of many kinds. People are losing their jobs, loved ones are dying, and our country is deeply divided along political lines. Suicide has become a public health epidemic, not just a personal problem. We cannot treat it like something that just happens and cannot be prevented. Whether we're healthcare providers, teachers, friends, or family members, we need to change our attitude toward the issue if we hope to reverse this alarming trend.

During the past couple of years, lockdowns in our own homes, financial chaos, marital pressure, and traumas affecting our children have taken a toll on all of us. Regardless of what the government may or may not do, the church should be a place of hope and acceptance. Survivors can be overwhelmed by feelings of anger and guilt because everyone seems to think they somehow could have prevented a suicide that happened in their family or among their acquaintances. Yet, here's the tough reality: suicide is impossible to predict.

Having faith in the Lord does not mean we can always handle life's unpredictability. Let us reduce the stigma of needing help for ourselves and our loved ones so we can pray and support one another. We need to provide resources for those struggling with mental illness so they do not face their demons alone.

If you or someone you love struggles with thoughts of suicide, please do not suffer alone. Get help from medical professionals, a local church, family, or friends. There is no shame in feeling helpless at times, but know that the Lord gives us no burden greater than what we can bear. Please seek the support of loved ones to pull you through and seek professional help where necessary.

THIRTY-TWO

Loving Our Neighbors

"This is the first and greatest commandment. And the second is like it: Love your neighbor as yourself."

—Matthew 22:38–39

As every Christian should know, feeling and demonstrating love for one another is a hallmark characteristic of our faith. Immediately after His instruction to love the Lord God with all our heart, soul, and mind—what He called the greatest commandment—Jesus gave the second greatest commandment: to love our neighbor as ourselves.

Is today's society really demonstrating that kind of love?

Sadly not.

Instead, we see a hardening of hearts, cruelty, and a callous disregard for life. These are not manifestations of people who love the Lord and their neighbors.

I know God is walking me through a season of learning what it truly means to be His disciple. A particularly menacing upheaval at our local school board was a lesson in grace and the power of prayer. After months of shouting matches, name-calling, and a lack of resolution on the most pressing issues, one parent invited everyone to a prayer circle after the meeting concluded. "We have done everything but pray." She was right, and it was time to call down God's mercy and healing.

The Lord showed me that despite our conflicts, the followers of Jesus must remember that the world is judging Christ by how we behave. We cannot control the actions of others, but we can control how we respond.

As someone who spent decades in the "works-based" religion of Islam, my immediate inclination was to try harder. If I could wake up each day intent on doing better, somehow, I would start to manifest His attributes of kindness, compassion, and, most of all, love. However, as a follower of Christ, I finally realized that striving in my own strength would never work. I soon learned that the starting point has to be with Him.

I knew God's greatest desire was for us to love Him and humanity with our whole hearts. It's a great way of being, but in practical terms, I did not understand *how*. Then I heard an excellent explanation from the pastor at my neighborhood church: The love of God is not based on emotions, and it is not something we can experience without the Holy Spirit. It is how a Christian draws closer to God through His Word and is transformed.

"Be Holy for your God is Holy."

—*1 Peter 1:16*

If we purify ourselves by obeying truth, we will love one another deeply from the wellspring in our hearts that emanates from God. We do not often hear holiness associated with love. Our instinct is to treat love as a transaction. We give love or withhold it because of how we feel toward a person or something they do or do not do for us.

"You have been born again, not of perishable seed, but of imperishable, through the living and enduring word of God."

—1 Peter 1:23

In other words, the love of God starts as that seed—a seed that the Spirit planted in us—that is nourished by the living Word. Though it's an indestructible seed, it can whither without nourishment. We cannot make it flourish independently, and the necessary amount of nourishment does not happen as we attend church once or twice a month. Deep, abiding love matures only when we spend time in the Scripture:

"As newborn babes, desire the spiritual milk of the word, that you may grow thereby…"

—1 Peter 2:2–3

We have to crave the Word and grow from the inside out. It is incumbent on us not just for our own lives but also because we are the first impression people get of God.

Unfortunately, though, believers are not reading the Bible nearly enough. A survey conducted in 2021 found that only 11 percent of Americans read the Bible daily, and the majority of Americans *never read the Bible at all*. As a result of those who are not familiar with the Word of God, churches are torn apart by internal conflict, and communities are riddled with hatred and malice.

If we find it hard to love one another, we need to ask ourselves if we are really saved.

"If someone says, 'I love God,' and hates his brother, he is a liar; for he who does not love his brother whom he has seen, how can he love God whom he has not seen?"

—1 John 4:20

Those are strong words, but they are *God's words*. He says them and exposes us to this reality for a reason. We need to evaluate our behavior and our collective actions as a church.

The God of the Bible is different from the false god of any other faith. He is a God who speaks. He relates to and communicates directly to His children through His Word. God breathes life into us and makes us that royal priesthood, people who love deeply despite all our differences or shortcomings.

I am still trying to fully grasp what it means to "love deeply," as Peter describes, but now I know the "how."

When I read the Bible cover to cover, I was struck by how many ideas rang true and were relatable thousands of years later. That was an awe-inspiring moment for me. The Bible is not simply words written down by men who were eyewitnesses to Jesus' ministry and wanted to give a historical account of His miracles.

> *"All Scripture is breathed out by God and profitable for teaching, for reproof, for correction, and for training in righteousness."*
>
> *—2 Timothy 3:16*

The Bible is God-breathed, infallible, and timeless. God has been talking to each and every one of us through His Word throughout the centuries. This is why it is almost a cliché at church each week that the pastor admonishes us to read it. It is not because he wants to give us homework. He knows it has the power to change us in a way no amount of service or charity ever could.

THIRTY-THREE

Where Are We Amidst the Chaos of the Ungodly?

"And for me, that utterance may be given to me, that I may open my mouth boldly to make known the mystery of the Gospel."

—Ephesians 6:19

The *Oxford Dictionary* defines chaos as "complete disorder and confusion." When used in physics, chaos is "behavior so unpredictable as to appear random."

One of the most stunning examples of chaos I've seen in a long time is how our society has treated law enforcement. Not long ago, there were two high-profile police shootings. In both, two armed individuals who were threatening the lives of the policemen were fatally shot.

In one of the instances, the officer was placed on administrative leave because he used his firearm, even though the suspect was armed and trying to outrun the police. In the other, the officer shot and killed a teenager who was poised to drive a knife into another person.

When all the smoke cleared, the harshest criticism was leveled against the *police* rather than the perpetrators. In fact, the media hosted numerous experts to explain how de-escalation tactics should have been used on the knife-wielding teenager since the young lady was a product of the foster care system and could not self-regulate her emotions.

It's *far* from the first time such a thing has happened, and given the state of our society, it also won't be the last.

To me, *that* is chaos.

Both the media and some politicians were quick to blame the police and reignite the passion for defunding police departments across the United States. Many are blind to the fact that defunding police has created a level of lawlessness that boggles the mind. Portland, Oregon, along with many other cities, dramatically reduced their police budgets with tragic consequences. Crime rates skyrocketed. Michigan Congresswoman Rashida Tlaib went so far as to post a public comment on Twitter that "policing in our country is inherently and intentionally racist. No more policing, incarceration, it can't be reformed." Her opinion left me speechless.

Every day, police officers have only seconds to make life-or-death decisions about threats to public safety, including immediate threats to their own lives. In my two decades of experience training and consulting for both local and federal law enforcement as I helped build early intervention programs for potential terrorists, if there was a real and credible threat of violence by an individual, other forms of intervention *were immediately ruled out.* The clear line of demarcation between community actors such as healthcare professionals and the police was when a person posed a physical threat to society. Multidisciplinary teams that can de-escalate a crisis are not utilized when there is a violent crime in progress. If the use of deadly force, carrying a weapon with the intent to use it, is no longer the standard for the role of law enforcement, chaos ensues.

That's right. *Chaos.*

God sets the standard of prohibiting violence and loving one's neighbor as yourself, as well as equity and justice for all in the sight of

God. We are taught forgiveness and compassion toward our enemies, and that vengeance belongs to the Lord. Our rule of law and respect for authority are based on these Biblical principles. Without a moral standard based on Biblical values, morality becomes relative.

Some claim that violence is justified to destroy systematic oppression or personal grievances, as we see when rioting breaks out in cities across the United States. At the same time, others decry the violence when their business is burned, or their home is attacked. Law and order will continue to decline if the use of violence is morally justified based on competing versions of social justice.

The most tragic aspect of this rise in moral relativism is that the church is almost entirely absent from the national dialogue. There are competing voices from conservative pundits and the liberal media, but we hear very little from the pulpit condemning the violence. Very few pastors are speaking and writing publicly to denounce the degradation of our societal norms. There are no national calls for repentance or for asking the Lord to intervene for His people.

Moses demanded that Pharaoh set the Israelites free, Elijah destroyed the prophets of Baal during the reign of King Ahab, and Daniel refused to bow in worship to King Nebuchadnezzar. God's elect *always* spoke truth to power when the power went against God's will for man. The Bible is not a series of fairy tales. It is God's living word to be used for instruction and teaching.

God's people can't sit idly by when lawlessness, evil, and violence run rampant. Under the new covenant with Christ, we no longer go to a physical temple. Our bodies are the temple of God to be used for repentance and prayer. The power of prayer is timeless. For example, we can use the prayer of Solomon in 2 Chronicles 6:12–42 as guidance in honoring God, repenting, and asking for blessing upon the land. It says [in part]:

> *"Lord my God, give attention to your servant's prayer and his plea for mercy. Hear the cry and the prayer that your servant is praying in your presence. . . . Forgive, and deal with everyone*

according to all they do, since you know their hearts (for you alone know the human heart), so that they will fear you and walk in obedience to you all the time they live in the land you gave our ancestors.

. . . When they sin against you—for there is no one who does not sin—and you become angry with them and give them over to the enemy . . . and if they have a change of heart in the land . . . and repent and plead with you . . . and if they turn back to you with all their heart and soul . . . then from Heaven, your dwelling place, hear their prayer and their pleas, and uphold their cause. And forgive your people, who have sinned against you."

In American history, George Washington and the Founding Fathers found strength in the preachers of the day who encouraged them to fight against the tyranny of the British. They believed it was their calling to set up a nation under God and that the church was there to support them from the pulpit. It was the little-known "black robe regiment" that provided the prayer and the word of God to support the revolution, not to mention soldiers who fought alongside them. The freedoms we enjoy today exist largely due to the support of the black robe regiment, who enshrined those beliefs in the nation's founding documents. Where is that regiment today?

The problem with the church, in many cases, is allegiances and alliances that are against God. Whether it is setting up false gods of fame and popularity or being afraid to confront the ungodly trends of the day, we are divided against ourselves. Jesus warns that:

"A city or house divided against itself, will not stand."

— Matthew 12:22–28

So, if we are unwilling to defend the truth of the Gospel, we may find ourselves irreparably lost like past generations until the remnant intercedes in a way that the Lord accepts (see Romans 11:5).

THIRTY-FOUR

Turning Away From Wickedness

"Since they thought it foolish to acknowledge God, He abandoned them to their foolish thinking and let them do things that should never be done. They have become filled with every kind of wickedness, evil, greed, and depravity."

—Romans 1:28–29

Chaos is a byproduct of depravity. Ultimately that depravity is rooted in disobedience and rebellion against God. When God is not the driving force in a society, evil takes over. It is as if the church woke up one day and found evil overtaking our families, communities, and our nation. The whole world is drowning in wickedness. We can't look to others to take care of it for us. As a church, we are the ones who must fight it with all our might.

In the book of Romans, the Apostle Paul wrote to a church that had just come out of a very depraved lifestyle. He was straightforward in his warnings, and because of what the church had so recently experienced, they understood. They could relate. *We can relate.*

It is astonishing how Paul's words still resonate more than 2,000 years later:

> *"So, God abandoned them to do whatever shameful things their hearts desired. As a result, they did vile and degrading things with each other's bodies. They traded the truth about God for a lie... Even the women turned against the natural way to have sex and instead indulged in sex with each other. And the men, instead of having normal sexual relations with women, burned with lust for each other. Men did shameful things with other men, and as a result of this sin, they suffered within themselves the penalty they deserved... They are backstabbers, haters of God, insolent, proud, and boastful. They invent new ways of sinning, and they disobey their parents. They refuse to understand, break their promises, are heartless, and have no mercy. They know God's justice requires that those who do these things deserve to die, yet they do them anyway. Worse yet, they encourage others to do them, too."*
>
> *—Romans 1:24-27, 30-32*

Our society has become shamefully similar to those in Paul's day—and the most alarming aspect of how similar we are is that "those that know the righteous decree" are either foolishly or knowingly supporting precisely the kind of immorality we are warned to avoid. Modern ideas of the "woke culture"—gender fluidity, same-sex relationships, and humanism (attaching more importance to human matters than to matters of God)—are *not* Biblical principles. According to the American Humanist Association, "Religious Humanism is without a god, without a belief in the supernatural, without a belief in an afterlife, and without a belief in a 'higher' source of moral values." How, then, can a Christian find common ground with such ideals?

On the opposite end of the spectrum, the Lord also commands the church to be one body, united in faith under one Spirit. However, unity is impossible without agreement. The body of Christ must be unified around the ultimate truth that is contained in the Bible. All of us have sinned and fallen short of God's ideals, but that does not mean that the church should condone immoral principles. All of humanity needs salvation—but salvation requires repentance from sin, the desire to turn away from it, and the acceptance of Christ as Lord and Savior.

These seemingly contradictory principles leave Christians with the difficult task of reconciling the commandment to avoid evil and the task of achieving unity within the body of Christ. We must be wise enough to distinguish between people simply acting foolish or naive instead of espousing wickedness. Being wise is not as the culture defines it; being wise in the ways of God means following His commands. Through knowledge of God's Word and prayer, we will gain the discernment and wisdom to know the difference.

Kids are being brainwashed to believe that if it feels good, they should do it. They are being taught there is no absolute truth—not relating to their gender, and not the notion of marriage only being between a man and a woman. They are being taught to reject the founding principles of our country.

Professors say you can't legislate morality, but you absolutely can! That is why we do not drive 100 miles per hour in a school zone, and it's why we do not condone photographing children in sexual activity (child pornography).

Morality isn't something you invent; it comes from God. Tacit support by the church of principles that stem from a denial of God's law leads to the destruction of our youth, our families, and eventually the moral fabric of our country.

Sometimes, believers follow trends in our culture out of ignorance. When such is the case, we extend grace and compassion to them—until it becomes clear they are unwilling to abandon their support of depravity. Other times, Christians have a hero mentality, thinking they can "save" people. It is critical to understand that some people *do not want to be saved.* They are filled with unresolved trauma, anger, and resentment that only the Lord can change if He so chooses. The Apostle Paul described what would happen in our day:

"There will be terrible times in the last days. People will be lovers of themselves, lovers of money, boastful, proud, abusive, disobedient to their parents, ungrateful, unholy, without love, unforgiving, slanderous, without self-control, brutal, not lovers of the good, treacherous, rash, conceited, lovers of pleasure rather than lovers of God—having a form of godliness but denying its power. Have nothing to do with such people."

—*2 Timothy 3:1–5*

Paul warns that the threat will come from those claiming a "form of godliness," but he does not say to pursue them relentlessly. We simply have to avoid them.

We should not be too proud of ourselves or so enamored with our civilization that we do not heed God's warnings. If we purposely or unwittingly accept modern principles that defy God's law, we will have a debased mind where God no longer reigns over our lives and the lives of our families and communities. Yes, we love our neighbors and pray for their salvation, but we cannot compromise the Gospel to please them.

— THIRTY-FIVE —

The Cult of Wokeism is Anti-American

At the heart of the turmoil unfolding in society lies what some have termed the cult of wokeism. This new wave of thinking has emerged as a sort of modern-day religion, capturing the attention and devotion of many.

This ideology, however, stands in stark contrast to the principles of Christianity. Left unchecked, it threatens to destabilize the very bedrock of American society. This isn't mere hyperbole; its aim is precisely that.

Perhaps the most unsettling facet of wokeism is its demand for absolute conformity. Those who question or reject its doctrines are quickly branded as ignorant, racist, and unworthy of social participation. It's an ultimatum—comply or face ostracism.

For those who hold fast to their Christian values, the path becomes even more treacherous, leading to possible alienation from their social circles.

Wokeism challenges existing power structures and seeks to dismantle what we have always accepted as universal truths. The United States is a nation shaped by the principle that "all men are created equal, that they are endowed by their Creator with certain unalienable rights, that among these are Life, Liberty and the pursuit of Happiness." These "self-evident truths" are from the preamble to the United States Declaration of Independence, which is the document on which our government and our identity as Americans are based.

Those words, with their accompanying sentiments, were written by our Founding Fathers. They were meant not only for that generation but for all who would inhabit the American continent. That includes all of us who are living here today.

Since many of the Founding Fathers were Christians, "the inalienable rights from the Creator" can be further expanded to include God's vision for man and society as told in the Bible:

> *"I charge you, in the sight of God and Christ Jesus and the elect angels, to keep these instructions without partiality and to do nothing out of favoritism."*
>
> —*1 Timothy 5:21*

> *"If you really keep the royal law found in Scripture, 'Love your neighbor as yourself,' you are doing right. But if you show favoritism, you sin and are convicted by the law as lawbreakers."*
>
> —*James 2:8–9*

Throughout our history, Americans have struggled with achieving these ideals. There has been some stumbling, as always, when people are working toward ideals. Still, through fierce debate, social turmoil, and even war, the outcome has been a continuous push toward achieving racial and gender equality, preserving individual liberty, and creating opportunities for economic prosperity. Together, our political leaders, civic activists, and the community at large have fought to dismantle institutional and legal systems that perpetuated racial or gender disparity. Due to these combined efforts, the United States is today one of the least prejudicial nations on earth.

That's the reality, but that's not how wokeism sees things at all.

Wokeism sees our nation as fraught with oppression from racial injustice and gender norms that overpower portions of our society and, therefore, must be destroyed. Through social media messaging, the opinions of celebrities, and even our politicians, their followers chant slogans demanding power for the people. They claim people are powerless based on a racial or ethnic class rather than their standing with God. They expect all of society to abolish traditional gender norms of males and females and assert that gender is a spectrum that the individual can self-determine. Their religion relies on control and power to impose their ideas, from which violence would be a natural consequence if people do not conform. Major corporations, politicians, and mainstream media are capitulating to these demands, so those who practice wokeism are able to remain relevant and avoid the persecution that comes from resistance.

Wokeism is far more effective than secularism ever could be because it fills the "God-shaped hole" in our culture. It claims its own interpretation of justice, righteousness, sin, and judgment. Followers find meaning in the ultimate goal of dismantling oppressive power structures to create their utopian society.

The ideas put forward by wokeism are the exact opposite of what God has repeatedly spoken to us as His children. We were created male and female; we were made in His image. We have authority over the earth and its creatures. We are told as such in Scripture:

> "Then God said, 'Let us make mankind in our image, in our likeness, so that they may rule over the fish in the sea and the birds in the sky, over the livestock and all the wild animals, and over all the creatures that move along the ground.' So, God created mankind in His own image, in the image of God He created them; male and female He created them."
>
> —Genesis 1:26–27

God instructs us to do what is right and to behave with justice, kindness, and love toward all, without favoritism or regard for race (see 1 Corinthians 12:13 and Acts 10:34–35). The avowed enemy of man is Satan, who comes to steal, kill, and destroy. If he can rob our society of faith in our systems of justice and freedom, he can replace it with whatever ideals he wants. Understood this way, wokeism at its core wants a war against God and everything God stands for. This makes Christians, who hold fast to God's law, the most formidable threat of all.

Our responsibility as followers of Christ is to uphold the standards set forth by God as the ultimate path to peace and justice in society. We should not capitulate to the divine order of the universe to be popular or liked, even with our family or friends. We can be tolerant of people who reject the truth, but we cannot compromise our belief in the existence of God's ultimate Truth. Jesus is the way, the truth, and the life (see John 14:6). There is no difference between us based on race:

> *"The same Lord is Lord of all and richly blesses all who call on Him."*
>
> —*Romans 10:12*

THIRTY-SIX

The Corruption
of the Language War

Another consequence of wokeism and moral relativism is that it can turn our government into a tool of its deception. Words, phrases, or even scientific facts are redefined in ways that are unpredictable and downright ridiculous. Ultimately, the confusion about simple terminology leads to civil strife. We enter the realm of language wars.

Here's a perfect example. The federal government issues periodic reports that detail the economic health of the nation. One that was released during the Biden administration was supposed to confirm whether America was formally in a recession.

However, that's not what happened.

Instead of taking responsibility for failed economic policies, the Biden administration chose to play word games. First, there was a horde of efforts to redefine *recession*. Exactly what constitutes recession? What are its markers? A slew of "experts" came on the mainstream media to convince the American people we were not really in a recession. They changed the formula, manipulated the data and all to what end? To trick the public into not blaming the government for the massive uptick in prices for groceries and gas at the pump. They wanted to come up with some other plausible explanation for why our paychecks no longer met our basic needs.

Ultimately, the technical definition of *recession* really does not matter to regular people who are struggling with white-hot inflation, steeply rising interest rates, difficulty in paying credit card debt and mortgages, and just plain staying afloat.

The administration's verbal gymnastics did nothing more than deny the country's dire economic predicament. In fact, they added insult to injury for thousands of American families suffering from the decreased value of their wages, soaring fuel costs, and skyrocketing food prices.

The principal method of human communication is a commonly understood language. It is how any society expresses shared meaning so its citizens can relate to one another. Any language war intentionally destroys that shared meaning in a conscious effort to reshape society.

Often a language war begins with misusing words or defining them based on the situation rather than an objective definition. For example, when there is a subjective interpretation of a word like *woman*, a whole new meaning is created. By separating gender from sex and allowing gender to be redefined based on circumstances, ties of mutual understanding are severed at the most basic level. We no longer have a healthy debate between opposing viewpoints on substantive issues because we are stuck fighting over the meaning of words. With our society's aggressive language wars, pronouns like *he* and *she* have become controversial.

There are plenty of examples of language wars that are raging right now. Consider, for instance, the terminology for an *illegal alien*, an expression that conveys a person's legal status upon entering the United States. Replacing *illegal aliens* with *undocumented immigrants* completely ignores the fact that the person committed a crime and illegally arrived in the United States. Redefining words does not cause harm *until* it's thrust upon a people and enforced through their laws, which is currently happening.

Those who are launching language wars do not have to rely on the judicial system when it can brainwash an entire population through mainstream media. They can change how people think and choose to describe even the simplest terms. Whether it's the word *woman* or a more complicated word and concept like *recession*, the ultimate goal is control. They want to tell us how to speak, and they have the overwhelming public support to punish those who refuse to play along.

However, civil discord is not the only consequence of this manipulation; there are also new victims and perpetrators. Anyone who refuses to accept these verbal adaptations is eventually labeled a racist, a homophobe, or even a terrorist. For example, according to recent updates in the *Merriam-Webster Dictionary*, you are a racist if you treat all people the same *because* you refuse to acknowledge the many racial inequities in society.

With all this weaponizing of words involving gender, sexuality, and race, it is not surprising that the church is also struggling with its place in this language war. For instance, removing male pronouns from certain verses of the Bible allows the church to avoid the controversy surrounding the discussion of traditional gender roles.

Here's an example:

> *"Be on the alert, stand firm in the faith, act like men, be strong. All that you do must be done in love."*
>
> —*1 Corinthians 16: 13-14*

The Greek word translated as "quit [act] you like men" is *andrizomai*, which is used just once in the New Testament and 25 times in the Septuagint (the Greek translation of the Old Testament). It is an imperative, a word of command that literally means "act like men."

Today's society wants to portray this trait as unfavorable and claims that men who are strong and courageous exude a form of "toxic masculinity" that is a detriment to society. As a result, homosexuality is normalized, and a man who indeed acts like a man is now abnormal—an oppressor. However, when the English translation of this verse is changed to "be courageous," our Bible teachers and pastors bypass the whole discussion of gender and focus on the quality of courage.

Ultimately, this is a detriment to the body of Christ, which should learn and discuss God's plan and purpose for each of the genders.

Another illustration of how linguistic manipulation is seeping into the Church is the recent update to the translation of *arsenokoitai* in 1 Corinthians 6:9 and 1 Timothy 1:10. Some versions of the Bible have changed the translation to read "men who engage in illicit sex" rather than "sodomites." Gay rights activists claim these verses prohibited temple prostitution and forced sex, not committed homosexual partnerships. The general editor for the 2021 edition of the NSRV bible claims the term *sodomites* was seriously misleading. Sadly, many others have adopted such views, which is why we see the worsening of such destructive trends.

God created human beings, and He created them as either male or female (see Genesis 1:27, 5:2; Matthew 19:4; Mark 10:6). A godly marriage is only possible between a biological man and a biological woman. Sexual acts between men and men, or women and women, are condemned by the holy Word of God (see Leviticus 18:22, 20:13; Romans 1:26–27; 1 Corinthians 6:9). These have been core, absolute teachings of the church for centuries, but the language war has opened them up for debate. Theologians, activists, and progressive pastors are changing the meaning of words in the Bible to fit the culture. Furthermore, the failure to articulate traditional Biblical gender roles may be one of the root causes of why some churches now accept same-sex marriages and the ordination of transgender or homosexual pastors.

All faithful Christians must recognize the times in which we live and fully ground ourselves in the authentic Biblical truth of God. The Apostle Paul warned us that many would follow a false gospel and believe in a "doctrine of demons." (see 1 Timothy 4:1). Changing the message of the Bible to suit the culture will only lead to inevitable, soul-destroying contamination—and will fulfill the prophecy Paul made millennia ago.

We know that Jesus said that whenever faithful believers were in the world, the world would be a place of hostility and persecution, not a zone of comfort. It sounds like we are right on track.

THIRTY-SEVEN

"White America" as Targets of Assault

"If the world hates you, you know that it has hated Me before it hated you."

—John 15:18

In light of all the woke, far-left agenda that is trying to remake our society, their biggest obstacle remains conservative Christians. We represent the only thing that stands between the wicked taking over entirely.

I use the phrase "White America" sarcastically since we are comprised of all ethnicities and races. We are united in our stand for Biblical and democratic values that are the foundation of our country. The radical left characterizes us as "angry white people" so they can garner support for the vilification of our principles as part of a broader scheme to undermine our way of life.

Whether it is a Syrian Muslim gunning down "Trump supporters" in Colorado or the attack near the Capitol by a Nation of Islam supporter, the conservative Christian community is under attack. The most dramatic example of this is the recent assassination attempt on Trump. Whether we want to blame it on the gross negligence of the Secret Service or other bureaucratic failures, the reality is that the hateful rhetoric against him and the MAGA extremists has reached a tipping point.

We must not look at each of these issues as separate unrelated events when each is a critical aspect of how insidious movements weaken traditional social structures. I researched and published extensively how nearly identical tactics are used by radical Islamists to transform the Middle East, South Asia, and now parts of Europe. For more than 50 years, radical Islamists have used outright violence, political upheaval, and large public campaigns to dramatically transform relatively tolerant societies into oppressive countries that eliminate personal liberties and remove the freedom to practice any religion other than radical Islam.

Most prominently, we see the results of their efforts in countries like Iran, Pakistan, Turkey, and Egypt, where Christians are either driven out entirely or suffer tremendous persecution. In Europe, I visited distinct neighborhoods in London and the Netherlands where non-Muslims are driven out, and the immigrants are so isolated from mainstream society that their communities seem to be parts of a foreign country.

These tactics are not limited to the Middle East and Europe. Islamists have engaged in similar campaigns here in the United States, successfully creating a group of homegrown terrorists and political organizations that seek to affect United States policy. Luckily, their efforts have remained marginal until now. The Judeo-Christian principles that govern American society and its legal system, coupled with a strong law enforcement apparatus, have been the bulwark against any ideological movement seeking to fundamentally change American society.

However, the assault on "White America" is uniting Islamists and the radical Left in a very dangerous new way. Recently, college campuses across the US have had massive protests against the Israeli war with HAMAS. After HAMAS brutally massacred over 1,000 Israeli citizens,

Israel vowed to end terrorism in the Palestinian territories. Since HAMAS hides weapons and soldiers among the civilian population, the civilian death toll has been, unfortunately, higher than expected. Again, that is the result of HAMAS having absolutely no regard for human life. They use their people as human shields. Suddenly, we see radical Left groups united with Islamists burning property, setting up encampments, and preventing Jewish kids from attending school due to fear of bodily harm.

Despite the property damage and persecution of the Jewish students, the White House has refused to take action. Very few arrests are ever made, and violence is rarely punished. The rise of anti-Jewish sentiment is even seeping over into the Christian community. No one should fool themselves that the Israel-Palestinian issue is separate from the assault on White America. The Jewish community is part of our country's founding heritage. The woke mob hates them as much as they hate us. It is hatred for God at its root.

These vigilantes can terrorize the population and do so with tacit support from some sectors of the federal government, local and state lawmakers, and a large portion of mainstream society. Together, the Islamists and the radical Left have the power to murder opponents *and* sabotage traditional legal and political structures.

Regardless of your personal opinion about Trump, the lawfare orchestrated against him and any powerful people who support him should terrify all of us. Utilizing the power of federal and state prosecutors to go after a political candidate for supposed crimes committed decades ago is unfair election interference. It is an attempt by those in power to thwart the will of the people. Every one of us should look at these cases—Steve Bannon, the owner of Telegraph, or Peter Navarro—and wonder what it would take for the government to come after me.

As anyone who has ever been in a legal battle can tell you, the greatest consequence of lawsuits is not who wins or loses but the emotional and financial drain of fighting them. Such legal battles create many opportunities for abuse. It is clearly a mechanism to harass and intimidate conservatives by dragging them into court and burying them in discovery, which eventually bankrupts them.

The orchestrated boycott and vilification of Georgia is another alarming example of how these movements operate. We have seen mainstream social structures—such as corporations like Coca-Cola, Major League Baseball, and even President Joe Biden himself—supporting the effort to isolate and punish Georgia for creating voting restrictions. The law, as enacted, protects the integrity of the voting system. However, the radical Left is trying to force the legislature to retract it by purposely mischaracterizing it as racial discrimination, which they hope will inflame the emotions of the public and cause financial harm.

The radical Left tried to use social and financial coercion to compromise the sanctity of how we vote in this country. The threat this poses to the future of America as we know it cannot be overstated. Just ask Venezuelans what happens when an ideological movement has the power to change political safeguards. The result is catastrophic.

Ideological movements like socialism, communism, or Islamism wear away at the fabric of a society in order to supplant it with a new and dominant ideology. This can be accomplished only by first dismantling the existing strongholds—traditional institutions like houses of worship, schools, political structures, and law enforcement. I have published reports detailing this phenomenon related to Pakistan, Southeast Asia, Egypt, and Europe—but I never thought I would see the same patterns gaining prominence in the United States, especially with the help of large portions of the American people. The alliance of the radical Left with Islamists is a dream come true for Islamists because it gives them a national platform and credibility that they would never have been able to achieve on their own.

There has never been a more critical time for Christians to defend our way of life. Not only are we facing physical violence at houses of worship or even at local convenience stores—but our law enforcement and political structures are at risk. Remember, the Lord warned us of such times when He said:

"Then they will deliver you up to tribulation and kill you, and you will be hated by all nations for My name's sake. And then many will be offended, will betray one another, and will hate one another. Then many false prophets will rise up and deceive many. And because lawlessness will abound, the love of many will grow cold."

—Matthew 24:9–11

We cannot ignore this assault on our way of life, and we must defend the values we believe in. The Apostles faced far worse than this in defense of the Gospel. They were persecuted, isolated, tortured, and even killed. They did not waiver because the Lord told them it would happen. They knew, as we should know now, that it was their obligation as Christ's followers to preach the Gospel so that others would be saved, regardless of the personal consequences.

"In fact, everyone who wants to live a godly life in Christ Jesus will be persecuted, while evildoers and impostors will go from bad to worse, deceiving and being deceived. But as for you, continue in what you have learned and have become convinced of . . ."

—2 Timothy 3:12–14

THIRTY-EIGHT

Eyes Wide Open

*"Do not be afraid.
Stand firm and you
will see the deliverance
the Lord will bring you
today. The Egyptians
you see today you
will never see again.
The Lord will fight
for you; you need only
to be still."*

—Exodus 14:13–14

Remember these words of Moses as he stood before the children of Israel on the shore of the Red Sea.

Considering all of our society's challenges, it is easy to become discouraged and want to give up. Yet, if we trust God to lead us through difficult times, He will do so. If we surrender to His will and open our hearts, we can walk according to our divine purpose and learn the wisdom He teaches us along the way.

This is as true for us today as it was for the Israelites thousands of years ago. The Lord *will* fight for us. In the end, He will make us victorious over our enemies— even when our enemies seem to present an impenetrable barrier.

However, we must fulfill our end of the bargain if we expect Him to help us.

Part of that, of course, is to be the best Christians we can be. We must evaluate our allies in this fight with eyes wide open. We cannot afford to be caught unaware by mistakenly regarding people, organizations, or corporations as allies when in reality, they do not stand for the values we cherish.

A good example is Chick-fil-A, the franchised chicken restaurant with over three thousand locations in forty-eight states, Puerto Rico, Canada, and Washington, D.C. For years, Chick-fil-A was considered to be a "safe" corporation that stood firm against the dangers being promulgated by the Left.

Too many were simply unaware. The deception could have continued indefinitely if not for social media exposure.

Social media recently exploded with the news that Chick-fil-A had officially gone over to the dark side by hiring a vice president of Diversity, Equity, and Inclusion (DEI), J. Patrick McReynolds. The uproar was not in reaction to McReynolds himself but to the establishment of DEI as an employment marker.

Here's the baffling part: No one knew why there was such uproar since McReynolds had been VP of DEI at Chick-fil-A since 2021. The pandemonium on social media was hardly breaking news. He was not a new hire but had been promoted within the company, where he had been employed since 2007.

The principles of DEI for Chick-fil-A are committing to be "Better Together" and to foster "mutual respect, understanding, and dignity everywhere we do business." On its face, that doesn't sound objectionable at all. However, DEI initiatives across hundreds of companies in the United States are simply a ruse for a highly discriminatory system that encourages racism instead of being a meritocracy. Quite simply, employees should be hired based on their qualifications to do a job, not their skin color. DEI values race over skills.

In the media blitz that erupted over DEI, the feeding frenzy over Chick-fil-A was on full steam ahead.

As several journalists pointed out, this was not a new phenomenon for the company. In fact, Chick-fil-A has been pandering to the woke mob for years—and a 2023 headline in the *Christian Post* read, "Chick-fil-A has been woke for years. You just didn't want to believe it." The article read in part:

"When the rest of the world lost its corporate marbles, conservatives liked to think that there was one place that would never let them down: Chick-fil-A. While other CEOs took their brands in wildly liberal directions, Christians took solace in the fact that at least one franchise could stand against the mob. Now, customers feel deeply betrayed. But the reality is, the chicken empire's capitulation started years before this."

Those of us who've watched Chick-fil-A up close know the company's moral compromise didn't happen overnight. For groups like Family Research Council, the bloom was off the nugget as far back as November of 2019 when, after years of holding the line, Chick-fil-A decided to put as much distance between Christians and their brand as possible.

To most people in the public square, the U-turn was completely unexpected."[10]

Check out some of the evidence that backs up the claims. In 2019, after years of pressure from LGBTQ groups, the company stopped funding the Salvation Army and the Fellowship of Christian Athletes. In 2020, the Chick-fil-A Foundation announced its new approach to charitable giving would focus on "nourishing the potential in every child" and donating to a smaller number of organizations focusing on education, homelessness, and hunger. Though it reframed how grants would be allocated, the Foundation did not expressly mention the LGBTQ controversy, nor did it exclude giving to faith-based charities in the future.

Back in 2019, *The Federalist* ran a story on how Chick-fil-A diverted its resources to organizations like Covenant House, which hosted drag queen story hour, and the Southern Poverty Law Center, which vilifies

---

[10] Suzanne Bowdey, "Chick-fil-A has been woke for years. You just didn't want to believe it," *Christian Post*, June 1, 2023.

conservatives with irrational hyperbole, accusing them of being white supremacists and racists.

As if those new programs were not enough evidence that Chick-fil-A is no longer the beacon of Christian values in corporate America, the problem may have been far more insidious.

In 2023, the Chick-fil-A Foundation funded a relatively small nonprofit called Elevate USA. Its mission is to build "long-term, life-changing relationships with urban youth, equipping them to thrive and contribute to their community." Elevate USA offers tutoring, mentoring, and other standard programs that serve at-risk youth.

All that sounds okay *until* you explore the organization's financing. Chick-fil-A has joined the murky underworld of the Silicon Valley liberal elites and their multi-billion-dollar nonprofit empire targeting conservative and Christian values in every sector of American society. Let me explain.

Elevate USA receives over 75 percent of its more than one-million-dollar funding from the Stand Together Foundation Inc. (Notice the similarity in the language to "Better Together" from the Chick-fil-A DEI page.) This foundation had over $140 million in annual funding for 2021, with more than $356 million in assets. A large chunk of their tax-free funding came from the National Philanthropic Trust, which had $9.4 billion in revenue in 2021 and nearly $16 billion in assets.

The funding ladder ultimately led to the Silicon Valley Community Foundation (SVCF), which accumulated more than $15 billion in assets in 2021. Though the average person would likely not notice that this web of organizations is related, it is a methodology well-known for terror financing or organized crime. Money laundering schemes are often hidden behind a complicated set of interlocking companies to mask the sinister nature of their activities.

The SVCF invests millions of dollars in the California Black Freedom Fund to intentionally provide unrestricted funds to nonprofits that advocate for public policy changes that "eradicate systemic and institutional racism." The California Black Freedom Fund was also generously supplied with grants from the Gates Foundation and JP

Morgan Chase, right after the 2020 riots to "build on the momentum" created during that time.

You read that right: they believe that the rioting and destruction of millions of dollars of personal property and government buildings in the summer of 2020 was a *momentum* they hoped to maintain and expand.

Despite its lofty goals and air of egalitarianism, the SVCF was slammed in the news for its toxic work culture and suspicious funding mechanisms. In addition to claims of workplace sexual harassment, unfair working conditions, and failure to serve local communities, SVCF became a repository for donor-advised funds (DAF) of wealthy Silicon Valley tech giants like Mark Zuckerberg. DAFs are basically legal fiction that allow donors to get a tax deduction for billions of dollars they give to a tax-exempt entity while still controlling how that money gets spent.

In other words, foundations like SVCF and the NPT are how Zuckerberg, Gates, and their buddies fund the massive effort to kill unborn babies, host drag shows for kids, and advocate for legislation that lets children castrate themselves without parental consent. These tech mob bosses have created and built thousands of small charities with the specific purpose of dismantling the foundational values of our society.

According to the *Chronicle of Philanthropy*, the biggest "charity" in the United States last year was not the United Way nor the Salvation Army. It was Fidelity Charitable, the not-for-profit arm of the mutual fund company where about 150,000 donors have DAFs, second only to the Gates Foundation. Fidelity gave its single largest donation of 2021, $141 million, to The Church of Jesus Christ of Latter-day Saints (previously known as the Mormons). Fidelity also contributes significantly to Planned Parenthood and the Salvation Army.

Chick-fil-A is the latest company in the crosshairs of furious conservatives calling for a boycott of popular companies like Budweiser and Target. However, what underscores their allegiance to this network of disingenuous evildoers masquerading as do-gooders is their betrayal of their loyal patrons. Chick-fil-A is a family-owned company, so it is not beholden to the ESG standards of publicly traded companies. They cannot pretend they were forced into this agenda. Their largest consumer base has always been the Christian community. Yet, they have been trying to appease the Left for more than a decade and have now caved to the pressure to fit in. It reminds me of the Biblical account of the prophet Lot: when faced with an angry mob that wanted to rape his angelic visitors, Lot offered his daughters instead. The fear of the angry mob can make human beings do dreadful things.

So, Chick-fil-A is not only woke; it has chosen the side of evil over the Christian community on whom they built their fortune. It's much worse than we thought. They have joined the soulless tycoons who sacrifice our children to this demonic agenda, warping their sense of self-identity in exchange for a lie. It is time that Christians call them out for their hypocrisy and remind them of the scriptural injunction:

> *"Do not be bound together with unbelievers; for what partnership have righteousness and lawlessness, or what fellowship has light with darkness?"*
>
> —*2 Corinthians 6:14*

It is time, too, for us as Christian conservatives to do whatever is necessary to protect our families and our society—which starts with keeping our eyes open.

GALLERY

President Donald J. Trump

Hedieh at Georgetown University

Mayor of Paris, Anne Hidalgo

Former President of Indonesia, Susilo Bambang Yudhoyono

Former President Barack Obama

Shaking hands with former President George W. Bush

Former Governor Pete Wilson and former President George Bush

Program launch at National Press Club

Former DHS Secretary Jeh Johnson

Designer Paloma Picasso

Simon Xavier Guerrand-Hermès, Vice Chairman, House of Hermès

King Charles of England

Mayor of the United Kingdom

Actor Lou Ferrigno

Donald Trump Jr.

Jack Hibbs
Pastor, Calvary Chapel Chino Hills
& President, Real Life Network

Former NRA spokesperson Dana Loesch

PART 5

THE POLITICAL BATTLE

"Then Jesus said to His disciples, 'Whoever wants to be my disciple must deny themselves and take up their cross and follow me. For whoever wants to save their life will lose it, but whoever loses their life for me will find it. What good will it be for someone to gain the whole world, yet forfeit their soul? Or what can anyone give in exchange for their soul?'"

—*Matthew 16:24–26*

— THIRTY-NINE —

America's Biblical Values

"For the glory of God, and advancement of the Christian Faith."—excerpt from the Mayflower Compact.

America has a long and cherished history of upholding Biblical values. The first settlers to come to this country, the pilgrims, crossed an ocean to escape persecution from the kings of Europe who imposed strict control over the church. Their desire as they began settling was to worship God freely.

Those early Americans envisioned a government accountable to the people but ultimately beholden to God's moral commandments. In November 1620, they penned what later became known as The Mayflower Compact—an outline of ideas that were later preserved in the United States Constitution. "We, in the presence of God, covenant ourselves into a civil body politic," they wrote.

They left nothing up to speculation. Their compact specified that their journey across the ocean was undertaken for their faith.

The settlers set up a congregational model of government, where the citizens convened to discuss societal matters under the auspices of God's law. In Greek, this congregational body is known as *Ekklesia*, the same word used in the New Testament for the church. When we say that our country is one nation under God, it's more than just an expression. It is an awareness that we will be accountable to Him for our actions.

In the 1600s, pastors and their churches formed cities and communities governed by laws based on their religious teachings. Pastor John Latham and his church founded Barnstable, Massachusetts. Pastor Roger Williams and his church—which later became the First Baptist Church in America—founded Providence, Rhode Island. Reverend John Wheelwright and his congregation founded Exeter, New Hampshire.

Pastor Thomas Hooker, a Puritan clergyman, founded Hartford, Connecticut, with his congregants. It was in 1638 that Pastor Hooker explained *in a sermon* that the foundation of government authority relied on the free consent of the people. The principles he preached became the Fundamental Orders of Connecticut, which was Connecticut's Constitution from 1639 until 1818.

In 1789, Frederick Augustus Muhlenberg, a Lutheran minister from a distinguished family in Pennsylvania, was elected the first speaker of the United States House of Representatives. Together with his brother John Peter, also a devoutly religious man, they passed the First Amendment in that first session of Congress, an amendment that guaranteed the freedom to worship as one wished and that the government would not restrict religious worship. Both gentlemen understood that the free exercise of their faith required protection from the potential abuse of federal power.

More than two hundred years later, that amendment stands today as the governing principle in guaranteeing America "shall make no law respecting an establishment of religion or prohibiting the free exercise thereof." More than two centuries later, we continue to protect what our first settlers saw as their God-given right.

The churches in this country formed themselves into a public state to preserve liberty and the purity of the Gospel of the Lord Jesus Christ. They created a form of governance that would best preserve the freedom to preach the Gospel. They found *no* inconsistency in securing their rights politically and living righteously. They also had no intention of removing the church from the state. Quite the contrary, they enacted laws to preserve religious liberty, not destroy it.

In his speech on the 150th anniversary of the signing of the Declaration of Independence, President Calvin Coolidge challenged all Americans:

> "It was early colonial clergy . . . [that] preached equality because they believed in the fatherhood of God and the brotherhood of man. They justified freedom by the text that we are all created in the divine image, all partakers of the divine spirit. Equality, liberty, popular sovereignty, the rights of man—these are . . . ideals. They have their source and their roots in religious convictions. Unless the faith of the American people in these religious convictions is to endure, the principles of our Declaration will perish. We cannot continue to enjoy the result if we neglect and abandon the cause."[11]

In our democratic republic, the people rule through their representatives. It is a responsibility we cannot dismiss nor ignore simply by saying we don't like politics.

From the beginning of time with Adam and Eve in the Garden, God has set clear moral standards for humanity. These standards were codified in law throughout the Old Testament. Though the people of Israel often failed to uphold those laws, God's expectations did not change. Severe punishment came upon the Israelites for their shortcomings and disobedience to the law. Christ's ultimate sacrifice meant Christians were no longer subject to the punishments outlined for violation of the law of Moses. However, God did not abolish ethical expectations on the believers.

---

[11] An abridgment of the speech is found at The Federalist Staff, "What Calvin Coolidge Said On The Declaration of Independence's 150th Anniversary," *The Federalist*, July 4, 2020.

Look at these few examples of how strongly the New Testament speaks about morality and sin. It's impossible to mistake the meanings of these passages:

> *"Whoever has my commandments and keeps them, he it is who loves me."*
>
> —*John 14:21*

> *"But if anyone causes one of these little ones who believe in Me to stumble, it would be better for him to have a large millstone hung around his neck and to be drowned in the depths of the sea."*
>
> —*Matthew 18:6*

> *"If your hand causes you to sin, cut it off. It is better for you to enter life crippled than to have two hands and go into hell, into the unquenchable fire."*
>
> —*Mark 9:43*

> *"Shall we sin because we are not under law but under grace? Certainly not! Do you not know that to whom you present yourselves slaves to obey, you are that one's slaves whom you obey, whether of sin leading to death, or of obedience leading to righteousness?"*
>
> —*Romans 6:15–16*

There is a tension in modern Christianity between those who do not engage in the affairs of the "kingdom of the world" because they are "citizens of Heaven" and those who believe divine citizenship is the reason to espouse righteousness here on earth. It is important to remember that the former led thousands of German Christians to stay tragically silent as the Nazis sent millions to the gas chamber. Then along came Dietrich Bonhoeffer.

A German Lutheran pastor, he founded the Confessing Church in opposition to Hitler's effort to combine all Protestant churches into a single pro-Nazi German Evangelical Church. Bonhoeffer refused to remain silent. He staunchly resisted the Nazi dictatorship, vocally opposing Hitler's genocide of the Jews. He was arrested and accused of being involved in a plot to assassinate Hitler. He was executed along with others who were charged with plotting the assassination during the collapse of the Nazi regime.

Silence in the face of sin is tacit acceptance. Christians must reach a consensus that prevents that kind of dangerous passivism from happening again.

Here in the United States, we now face formerly unimaginable laws. Imprisoning parents who do not consent to the sexual mutilation of their children. The establishment and codification of more than fifty genders. The murder of unwanted babies, even *at birth*. The government imposition of medical treatments that alter our God-given genetic composition. How many more abominations will it take to reach that tipping point that demands all Christians speak out?

Recall the Lord's impassioned warning to the church at Thyatira:

> *"I have a few things against you, because you allow that woman Jezebel . . . to teach and seduce My servants to commit sexual immorality. . . . I gave her time to repent of her sexual immorality, and she did not repent. Indeed, I will cast her into a sickbed, and those who commit adultery with her into great tribulation, unless they repent of their deeds . . . and all the churches shall know that I am He who searches the minds and hearts. And I will give to each one of you according to your works."*
>
> —*Revelation 2:20–23*

Those powerful words and sentiments were not just for the church at Thyatira. They are for us, too, and we would be wise to heed them with all our might.

Regardless of how lost or debased the actions of our leaders may be, every believer is personally accountable to God for preserving His commandments. This obligation also includes protecting freedom of speech, religious liberty, and the moral imperative to be a voice for the voiceless.

If believers choose not to obey God, His people will be held to account for silence or inaction in the face of disobedience and sin. That's not just a theory. God Himself has said it throughout Scripture. It will be a rude awakening for church members who think they are spiritual by not getting involved when they wake up and realize that by their silence, they gave consent to sin.

Someday, all of us will die. What are people going to say about each of us? Did you or I let the fear of man stop us from doing what we needed for God?

Imagine this is a basketball game. Jesus is the coach, and you're on the bench. He comes over, looks you directly in the eye, and says, "Okay, your turn; get in the game."

You answer, "But they're playing really tough out there."

"Yeah, I know. It's your turn. Get in the game. You're seven feet tall. Those players on the other team are four feet tall. You can do this. They may be rough, but nothing they try against you will prosper because I am in you."

Out of the last 6,000 years of recorded human history, the Lord designated that you would be alive *right now*. This is your chance to shine and do great things as the child of God you are. We still have breath in our lungs. We can still do the things for which we will be known forever.

FORTY

Faith in Politics

"For I am not ashamed of the Gospel of Christ, for it is the power of God to salvation for everyone who believes."

—Romans 1:16

Some would say my enthusiasm for the Lord stems from being a relatively new Christian. Personally, I don't think that's the only reason. I had the opportunity to hear from former United States Secretary of State Mike Pompeo, who spoke at our church. He made it so clear why all Americans should be passionate about professing our faith.

Mr. Pompeo talked about being an openly devout Christian while he served as Secretary of State. His faith informed all he did. He was often asked, "How does being a Christian impact your life?" He knew the question was meant to be negative, but he said the negativity was irrelevant to him. He responded with conviction and shared these words:

"[Your faith] impacts everything you do; it informs every action that you take. It impacts how you think about the world, how you interact with people, and every day in your work life. Our founders believed deeply this was right and that the capacity to exercise our religion freely was important, and it mattered. . . . My oath was to the nation, I raised my right hand and swore that I would support and defend the American Constitution, but I knew that if I did that with the Lord in my heart, I'd be more successful at delivering on that very outcome."

Whether it was President Abdel Fattah el-Sisi in Egypt or Supreme Leader Kim Jong Un of North Korea, world leaders respected Secretary Pompeo for his belief, and there is nothing un-American or unbiblical about it. In his seminal speech in Cairo, he began his remarks by saying, "I'm Mike Pompeo, and I'm an evangelical Christian." His speechwriters tried to remove that statement, but he insisted on retaining it. He knew it was essential not because he wanted to talk about Christianity in a Muslim nation, but because he wanted them to understand that believers of Christ wanted good things for people everywhere and that it's our responsibility to be faithful, no matter where we are.

Even to this day, there is not one line about which he gets more questions or comments. Leaders of every faith worldwide—Christians, Jews, and Muslims—say they appreciated his honesty. They appreciated that he kept faith in the public square. They admired the discipline with which he practiced his faith. They appreciated his courage to talk about his values so they could better understand how our nations could work together to deliver better lives for people across the globe.

Some officials in the United States criticized his openness, but that criticism never deterred him. Unfortunately, many government representatives wrongly interpret the First Amendment as prohibiting talking about faith, but it does not. Freedom of religion is meant to protect the rights of people of all faiths and allow them to practice their religion without encroachment from the government.

In my experience, disastrous policy decisions have stemmed from a lack of religious conviction in US government officials. I will never forget being in a closed-door meeting at the White House during the Obama administration, where a small group of us was invited to address the president on "countering violent extremism." After nearly an hour of our passionate pleas and recommendations for stricter policies toward state sponsors of terrorism and other stringent measures, the president said he didn't "get religion" and would not let people drag him into a war over it.

Quite frankly, this sentiment explains why he did virtually nothing about the explosion of violence in the Middle East during his tenure.

Suppose many of our senior U.S. diplomats cannot appreciate the impact religion has on the way people live their lives and determine their priorities. How can we then properly represent our country as a nation founded on Judeo-Christian values?

Secretary Pompeo went on to say, "There's no separation between faith and country because God governs in the affairs of men. Our success depends on virtuous people. Wherever that is— volunteering in the parking lot at church or serving in government—our faith should form our character and inform our opinions."

Being a Christian should be part of whatever we do. That doesn't mean we are trying to convert people. It simply means that we—and people of all other faiths—should be able to freely practice whatever religion we believe in. If our faith is not public and visible, how can we call others to faith in Christ? It is not just about being a good person.

> *"How then shall they call on Him in whom they have not believed? And how shall they believe in Him of whom they have not heard? And how shall they hear without a preacher?"*
>
> —*Romans 10:14*

I am eternally grateful for receiving salvation after practicing Islam freely in the United States for decades. I also cherish the freedom to share my new faith with others.

FORTY-ONE

What Good Can Come
From War?

War isn't something we usually associate with good. Instead, we normally talk about war in terms of the cost—not only in economic terms but in lives lost and widespread destruction.

Here's an excellent example of a war that's not very far off the radar. The nearly two decades of America's "combat mission" in Afghanistan— our nation's longest war—has been dubbed the "forever war." More than 6,000 Americans lost their lives, and almost $1 trillion U.S. taxpayer dollars were spent. Yet there's little to show for it politically or economically.

However, the war didn't seem to strike a chord with the average American despite its long duration and hefty cost. An Associated Press writer noted in *U.S. News and World Report*: "Ordinary Americans tended to forget about it, and it received significantly less oversight from Congress than the Vietnam War. With a death toll in the tens of thousands, generations of Americans will continue to shoulder the burden of paying it off."[12]

---

[12] https://apnews.com/article/middle-east-government-and-politics-afghanistan-fa04222 3d4943191910963026f2c2123

It might seem like the two decades spent in Afghanistan were entirely in vain.

But that's not the whole story.

The investment of American resources and political will did yield two significant benefits. Firstly, it championed the advancement of women and girls in what was a severely repressive Islamic state. Secondly, it introduced innovative methods to spread the Gospel of Christ in a region where Christianity was previously unwelcome.

I had the unique opportunity to serve as a political advisor at the U.S. Embassy in Afghanistan in 2004. My mission was to help build a civil society infrastructure that could resist the Taliban's radical Islamic agenda and their indoctrination of the youth. With ample financial support from American agencies, nonprofits, and even foreign allies, we set out to establish new institutions. However, we soon discovered that our greatest challenges were mismanagement, security threats, and rampant corruption.

It felt like a constant whirlwind of pandemonium. Americans were eager to complete their mission, yet endless setbacks made real progress seem impossible. I'll never forget a staff meeting where USAID representatives proudly presented a "newly built" school in one of Afghanistan's most dangerous regions. Midway through their impressive PowerPoint, a senior U.S. diplomat, originally from Afghanistan, erupted in anger. According to him, this school didn't exist! He had just flown by helicopter days earlier, investigating claims of deceit and corruption from our Afghan partners.

The USAID presenter looked stunned and bewildered. Clearly, he hadn't meant to deceive anyone. Most parts of Afghanistan were too dangerous to visit directly, so they relied on data from foreign allies, locals, and contractors who had their own motives to stretch the truth. Additionally, development projects needed multi-million-dollar private security just to operate. Ironically, much of that money ended up in the hands of the Taliban, who were the source of these security issues.

You know the old saying: the road to hell is paved with good intentions.

Yet, there were silver linings. Billions may have been lost to corrupt contractors, inefficient aid organizations, and bureaucratic red tape, but there was tangible progress in empowering Afghan women. For the first time in decades, Afghan girls were back in school. Jobs and networking opportunities flourished for articulate, brave Afghan women through international organizations. Even though the eventual withdrawal from Afghanistan destroyed many of these efforts, no one could erase the skills and knowledge these women had gained.

I frequently spoke at national and international events on defeating Islamic radicalism and building civic institutions, encouraging these incredible women. Their willingness to risk everything for freedom and a better future always moved me. Americans should take pride in the opportunities we created despite our blunders. It might be these very women who pose the greatest threat to the Taliban's plans to reinstate draconian laws.

My time and experiences in Afghanistan happened while I was a practicing Muslim, but now, as a follower of Christ, my views have changed. Like many who invested time and resources into political and social change, I was disappointed in our failures. Yet, my hope lies in the seeds of faith in Christ that were planted. Active Christian missionary work was forbidden, and even owning a physical Bible was risky. Despite this, the underground church grew as small groups met in private homes. One report mentioned, "Mullahs have come to Christ through supernatural means, leading hundreds of followers. Some former Taliban members who found forgiveness and new life in Christ are risking death to share their faith with other Taliban fighters and leaders."[13]

---

[13] https://www.ipcprayer.org/en/ipc-connections/item/10832-afghanistan-a-nation-where-christ-s-church-is-growing.html

The most impactful evangelism, however, came through the internet and social media. Due to the international presence, powerful internet capabilities were established, and these became crucial channels for spreading the Gospel. Isik Abla, a former Muslim, noted that some of her ministry's most significant Facebook engagements were from Kabul.

I'm not surprised by the internet's power in reaching Afghans—it's how I found Christ. I never stepped into a church or had Christian friends to guide me—Christ found me through a screen.

If you ever doubt that Christ can reach anyone, anywhere, think again. The Lord reveals Himself in the most extraordinary ways to those seeking truth. I have many former Muslim friends, including an Afghan woman, who experienced miraculous encounters with Christ, bringing them to faith despite immense risks.

So, even though the U.S. troop withdrawal from Afghanistan is a regrettable chapter filled with failures and miscalculations, we should celebrate the victories for women's rights and the spread of the Gospel. These forces might just reshape Afghanistan's future.

FORTY-TWO

Christian Persecution Worldwide

Since the International Religious Freedom Act was enacted in 1998, the U.S. has made promoting religious freedom a key aspect of its foreign policy. This law created an ambassador-at-large for religious freedom and an independent commission to advocate for persecuted religious communities, with the power to penalize offending nations.

The United Nations Ambassador, Linda Thomas-Greenfield, promised to improve diplomacy on pressing global issues, emphasizing a recommitment to defending democracy and human rights for all. As admirable as that sounds, her commitment to defending Christians against persecution is noticeably absent. Despite her stated goals, it seems unlikely she will use her diplomatic influence to champion this cause.

I worked in Washington, D.C. policy circles since the beginning of the Religious Freedom Commission. I participated in numerous discussions, conducted research, and traveled on behalf of the U.S. State Department to address these issues. Ironically, the U.S. focus was often more on protecting the rights of radical Islamists rather than expanding protections for Christians. Even as a Muslim at the time, this troubled me deeply, as it allowed Islamic extremists to gain prominence and led to increased terrorism.

During the Obama administration, emphasis on religious freedom diminished in favor of LGBTQ issues, leaving the Ambassador-at-Large position vacant for over two years. Ambassador Thomas-Greenfield has since reduced funding to agencies in Uganda and Nigeria that discriminated against the LGBTQ community.

A shift came during the Trump administration when former Secretary of State Mike Pompeo elevated the Office of Religious Freedom to report directly to the Undersecretary for Civilian Security, Democracy, and Human Rights and the Ambassador-at-Large to report directly to the Secretary of State.

Commissioners testified before Congress on the plight of Christians in Africa and the Middle East, calling for stricter policies. Former U.N. Ambassador Nikki Haley championed the cause of persecuted Christians in the Middle East and India, and U.S. diplomatic pressure notably improved conditions for Christians in Egypt and Saudi Arabia.

Under the Biden administration, some liberal Christian groups still hoped international religious freedom would be emphasized. Still, many conservative Christians doubt there will be any pressure on Muslim nations to protect Christian minorities.

Ambassador Thomas-Greenfield's remarks indicate grim prospects. At the U.N. General Assembly's commemoration of the International Day for the Elimination of Racial Discrimination, she criticized China and Myanmar for genocide against Muslim minorities. Afterward, she shifted focus to U.S. racism, emphasizing dismantling white supremacy and notably omitting the persecution of Christians.

Without the U.S. leading diplomatic efforts to protect minority Christian communities, their lives are at grave risk. More than 340 million Christians face high levels of persecution and discrimination, with deaths increasing by over 60% since 2021. If Thomas-Greenfield's first official speech is any indication, Christian persecution could even escalate within the United States.

In another part of the world, relations between Armenia and Turkey have remained hostile due to the mass killings of Armenians by

Ottoman Turks over a century ago. Historians mark those events as the first genocide of the 20th century, which Turkey vehemently denies.

Unfortunately, the brutal killing of Armenians continues until today. In a little-known part of the globe, the world's oldest Christian community is literally being starved to death. The Nagorno-Karabakh region has long been a place of religious and ethnic strife. In 2020, a significant and deadly escalation of a long-standing dispute between Armenia and Azerbaijan over this region occurred. As a result, both sides suffered significant casualties and territorial changes. Though the region is internationally recognized as part of Azerbaijan, it has a predominantly ethnic Armenian population. The two countries have warred over this territory since the early 20th century, but it became particularly intense after the dissolution of the Soviet Union.

Russia brokered a ceasefire agreement between the two parties in November 2020 and deployed Russian peacekeeping troops to monitor the situation and maintain the ceasefire. However, it is no surprise that while Russia is now engrossed in its battle with Ukraine, its troops are no longer monitoring this region. Meanwhile, the Azeri government uses it as an opportunity to finish what it started back in 2020. Beginning in July 2023, Azerbaijan has blockaded the only road to the region known as the Lachin Corridor, causing dwindling food, medicine, and electricity.

Turkey, a NATO member with longings for increased global influence, supports its longtime ally Azerbaijan on the battlefield or at the negotiating table against the Armenians. Turkey and Azerbaijan have strong ethnic and cultural ties, including their religious affiliation with Islam. The two nations also have strong economic ties, including oil and gas exports, large-scale military training, and arms sales together. In solidarity with Azerbaijan, Turkey has no diplomatic relations with Armenia and sealed its border with the nation in 1993.

Although Russia and Armenia do not share a border, Armenia is a close ally of Russia, including hosting a large Russian military base. With a garrison of about 3,000 soldiers, the base is characterized as a critical barricade against a possible Turkish invasion. With Russia largely distracted by its turmoil with Ukraine, it leaves this embattled community of Armenian Christians at the mercy of its aggressive Muslim neighbors. Ultimately, the goal appears to be eradicating this ancient Christian population like many other Muslim-majority countries have done throughout the Middle East.

The crisis in Nagorno-Karabakh has far-reaching consequences for the rest of the world as well. The Arab Christian communities have a rich history that dates back to the early days of Christianity. They have been integral to the Middle East's social fabric for centuries. With roots tracing back to the birthplace of Christianity, these communities have played significant roles in national culture, education, and politics. However, in the aftermath of the endless warfare in the Middle East and North Africa, these communities have faced unprecedented challenges and destruction.

It started with the invasion of Iraq in 2003 and spread throughout the world in what we called the "Arab Spring." U.S. policymakers had this lofty notion that these countries would easily evolve into bastions of freedom if only the West could liberate them from oppressive dictatorships. Though the idea sounded appealing, it was naive and impossible to impose or create by external forces. The indigenous forces saw the Western nations as occupiers and invaders.

Revolutions in Libya, Egypt, and Tunisia, as well as uprisings in Iraq, Syria, and Lebanon, led to guerilla warfare on the Arab streets. The breakdown of law and order created an environment where extremist groups flourished, leading to violence against religious minorities, especially Arab Christians. Islamic extremist networks rose in prominence and gained control in many parts of the world. Naturally, the civil war in these countries quickly turned religious, and Arab Christians often found themselves caught in the crossfire. As suspicions grew, Arab Christians faced discrimination and persecution, with their religious identity becoming a source of suspicion.

Fearing for their safety, a significant number of Arab Christians chose to leave their ancestral homelands in search of safety and opportunities elsewhere. This mass migration has led to the dwindling of once-vibrant Christian communities in the Middle East. Churches and religious sites have not been spared either. Throughout the region, countless churches have been damaged or destroyed due to conflict, leaving Arab Christians without places of worship and symbols of their faith. In addition to the physical threats they face, Arab Christian communities have also suffered economically. The breakdown of stability in their regions has disrupted their livelihoods, leading to unemployment and poverty.

The destruction of Christian communities like Nagorno-Karabakh is a tragedy with profound consequences. These communities, which have preserved their faith and heritage for centuries, are now facing extinction in many parts of Asia, the Middle East, and Africa.

Unfortunately, the U.S. and our European allies have done little to protect their fledging communities. The UN makes statements calling for the end of the blockade or criticizing the attacks, but no real effort is made to threaten the aggressors with sanctions or other diplomatic consequences. Efforts must be made at both the international and local levels to protect and support these vulnerable communities. This includes addressing the root causes of instability, promoting religious tolerance, and providing assistance to those who have been displaced. Preserving Arab Christian communities is not only a matter of cultural and religious heritage but is a testament to the importance of coexistence in a world that is increasingly less tolerant and diverse.

FORTY-THREE

Religious Freedom in Crisis

It is not an accident or coincidence that the free exercise of religion is the first right bestowed in the United States Constitution. The Founding Fathers knew a government centered on the supremacy of God and man's obedience to His commandments would make America exceptional.

American Christians know the "God first" policy is much older than any presidential administration or chapter of American history. The Lord Himself says:

> *"The most important one,"
> answered Jesus, "is this: ...Love the
> Lord your God with all your heart
> and with all your soul and with
> all your mind and with all your
> strength."*
>
> *—Mark 12:29-30*

When we love God with everything we have, it is the well from which we draw love for everyone around us. It is the essence of justice because there is no discrimination based on race or religion, no judgment of right or wrong; there is simply the love for humanity emanating from our love of God. It is not meant to be exclusionary or intolerant; it is how we manifest the fruits of the Spirit—kindness, goodness, forbearance, and self-control.

As Christians, we are always representations of Him:

> *"Therefore, we are ambassadors for Christ, as though God were making an appeal through us, we beg you on behalf of Christ, be reconciled to God."*
>
> *—2 Corinthians 5:20*

We also protect and defend religious liberty as a guiding principle of American foreign policy—not because it is a campaign slogan for one side of the political divide, but because it is the morally right thing to do.

The Biden administration championed the *interdependence* of human rights, making religious freedom just one of many democratic rights balanced with competing interests. America hasn't always seen it that way. Previously, religious liberty was considered the first right from which all others flow. Former Secretary of State Mike Pompeo made sure religious persecution of Christians was at the forefront of his foreign policy, and world leaders knew it would be a central part of the diplomatic negotiations.

Unfortunately, today's world is not a friendly or safe place for people of faith, especially when that faith is Christianity.

If you think that statement is too bold, let's look at a few examples from the world community. Let's start with Nigeria—referred to by Genocide Watch as "a killing field of defenseless Christians." The ethnic Fulani militants are considered the world's deadliest terrorist group, wiping out entire Christian villages while leaving Muslim villages unharmed. The central government's failure to protect the Christians demonstrates a gross violation of religious freedom. Open Doors USA, an organization serving persecuted Christians in more than 70 nations, has "documented thousands of targeted killings of Nigerian Christians every year for more than a decade," according to CEO David Curry.

Until very recently, Nigeria was designated as a "Country of Particular Concern"—a term used by the U.S. State Department for nations that are among the world's most egregious violators of religious freedom. Astonishingly, Nigeria has now been removed from the list. Open Doors USA lists Nigeria as ninth among the world's top 50 persecutors of Christians. Open Doors senior fellow Sam Brownback, formerly the US Ambassador-at-Large for International Religious Freedom under Trump, said that removing Nigeria from the list of most egregious violators "rewards the Nigerian government for tolerating severe religious freedom violations and sends a message to extremists that their actions will continue to go unpunished. People of faith in Nigeria will bear the fallout of this decision, and that's unacceptable."

Russia replaced Nigeria on the list. Other designated countries of particular concern are China, Eritrea, Iran, North Korea, Pakistan, Saudi Arabia, Tajikistan, Turkmenistan, and Myanmar (called Burma on the list).

There's also a "Special Watch List" —a list of runner-up nations with significant violations of religious freedom. That list includes Algeria, Comoros, Cuba, and Nicaragua.

Nine militant groups also have been designated as "Entities of Particular Concern": al-Shabab, Boko Haram, Hayat Tahrir al-Sham, the Houthis, the Islamic State group (ISIS), ISIS-Greater Sahara, ISIS-West Africa (ISWAP), Jamaat Nasr al-Islam wal Muslimin, and the Taliban. It goes without saying that these groups are not restricted to any one geographic location. The challenges to religious freedom today are not just structural and systemic; they are a profound injustice that pierces the heart of humanity.

The widespread persecution of Christians isn't limited to nations designated as especially egregious. Turkey and Azerbaijan renewed their aggression against their Christian neighbor, Armenia, timing the assault to coincide with the 100th anniversary of the Armenian genocide. They attacked Armenian churches and cultural heritage sites, sending a strong message that the war was not just about land but about faith. Sadly, the United States approved millions of dollars in new military aid to Azerbaijan without assurance they would stop the assault on Armenia. That tacit support emboldened Azerbaijan, which then sent troops and invaded Armenia proper, killing more than a dozen Christians.

In Afghanistan, the Taliban is going door-to-door, executing Christians on the spot. They also demand to see the cell phones of people using public transportation; anyone who has a Bible on their phone may be executed on the spot.

According to Open Doors USA, more than 340 million Christians cope with persecution on a daily basis. Fifty countries—primarily in the Middle East, Africa, or Asia—have very high levels of persecution. What that means is that one out of every eight Christians faces severe consequences based solely on their faith.

While not everyone may impact religious freedom globally, each of us holds incredible power to spotlight the persecution of Christians. Through the force of our words on social media and personal networks, we can awaken hearts and minds to this urgent crisis. By passionately advocating to our lawmakers, we urge them to enforce stronger penalties on nations ignoring their Christian minorities. It's up to us to make this a priority, pushing elected officials to recognize and act on this tragedy. Together, we can drive change and bring justice to those suffering in silence.

FORTY-FOUR

Don't Ban Free Speech!

Over the past several decades, the U.S. Department of State has spent millions of dollars expanding digital technology to promote free expression and democratic elections and reduce the threat of online Islamic radicalization. I served as a subject matter expert on several of those programs, providing quality control and oversight on whether the programs were achieving their intended outcomes. It was a dangerous field, with trips often delayed by terror threats and other unforeseen travel hazards. On one of the projects expanding the use of internet technology in Iran (based in Lebanon), my colleague was imprisoned and charged with espionage. Contractors, aid workers, and diplomats alike accepted the risks because we believed in the inherent value of free speech to defeat tyranny and promote democratic values.

Remember all the color revolutions that swept throughout the Middle East and North Africa? There were large-scale demonstrations on the streets, with demands for free elections or regime change and calls for removing authoritarian leaders. Many of those would not be possible without the technical support of the U.S. and other Western countries. They gave everyday citizens the ability and know-how to propagate information online that mobilized thousands of supporters. The dissemination of ideas about government corruption, abuse of political dissidents, and the innate human desire for freedom ultimately prevailed in many of those nations. Their triumphs were a victory for democratic ideals, regardless of ethnicity or religion.

However, the standing of the U.S. and its allies as the beacons of freedom is eroding. The obsession with combatting "(mis) disinformation" and the lack of respect for differing political opinions is having a dangerous ripple effect on other regimes seeking to consolidate power. Taking a cue from our rhetoric, countries like Tunisia, Turkey, and Russia, have sought to criminalize "disinformation" to silence journalists and their political opponents.

In Turkey, their new disinformation bill censors online information content and criminalizes journalism deemed false or misleading. It empowered the government to further subdue and control public debate in the lead-up to Turkey's general elections in 2023. It is considered one of the heaviest censorship mechanisms in the history of the Republic.

In Tunisia, the law imposes harsh criminal penalties for the intentional distribution of information that appears to "promote, publish, transmit or prepare false news, statements, rumors or documents that are artificial…"

Less surprising is Russia's recent amendment to its 2019 disinformation law that imposes up to 15 years in prison for anyone publishing information about the Russian armed forces that is deemed to be "false" or said to have "discredited" them.

Even the European Union, which advised against criminalizing disinformation as recently as 2017, has now proposed a new framework that imposes sanctions and freezes the assets of those who "spread information intended to manipulate or mislead."

In the West, the whole idea of banning bad ideas or even outlandish conspiracy theories has never been grounds for criminal prosecution. However, since the 2016 presidential campaign and the Russian spread of propaganda to influence our elections, this idea of criminalizing speech has gained momentum. The United States has long been the master of information wars in our struggles to defeat Communism. We fought destructive ideas with better ones focused on freedom and the right to self-determination. U.S. national security also includes intelligence operations that prevent foreign government attempts to undermine our way of life. But that's a far cry from arresting fellow Americans because their ideas against vaccinations are too dangerous or their political views are controversial.

Public statements by left-leaning government officials and interviews in mainstream media hammer home the idea of stopping any speech it doesn't agree with. Reporters now describe our constitutional protection of speech as a "challenge" to overcome rather than the cherished freedom we promote worldwide.

Thankfully, the First Amendment remains a bulwark against overt attempts to criminalize unpopular speech here in the US. However, several whistleblowers claim the FBI "has been manipulating case-file management to falsely inflate the threat of domestic terrorism and using unconstitutional excessive force against political dissenters."[14] This is an alarming accusation and severely undermines public confidence in how law enforcement is being used to silence political opposition.

Though on its face, one can find justification for preventing the widespread use of false information, the obvious question becomes who defines what is false. The FBI accusations illustrate how opinions can be weaponized and have serious consequences. Some experts suggest solutions such as reinvigorating civics education in schools and through public information campaigns to restore trust in our voting process, the judiciary, and law enforcement. Such programs would have the dual benefit of educating our populace and increasing transparency in our systems of government.

---

[14] https://nypost.com/2022/09/28/30-ex-fbi-agents-stand-up-to-support-whistleblower-who-exposed-agencys-political-bias/

Ultimately, as Americans, we cannot stop leading by example. Our laws and policies should demonstrate that we trust the free marketplace of ideas. Otherwise, the U.S. government's paranoia and overreach to stop the free flow of information will be why other nations oppress, harass, and curtail the freedoms we fought so hard to promote.

FORTY-FIVE

Be Wary of the Thought Police

*"For the wrath
of God is revealed
from Heaven against
all ungodliness and
unrighteousness
of men who suppress
the truth in
unrighteousness."*

—Romans 1:18

Our rights to free speech and religious freedom aren't just under threat abroad; they're in danger right here at home. The Department of Homeland Security (DHS) recently tried to set up a Disinformation Governance Board to keep tabs on "disinformation." Although public backlash quickly shut it down, this was a disturbing move away from our Constitutional values. In my experience with government counterterrorism, the battle between protecting free speech and combating radicalization was nothing short of harrowing. Watching young Americans leave their families to marry strangers or perish in distant wars is a heart-wrenching tragedy, driven by the manipulative words of persuasive recruiters. Our hands were tied, unable to act legally because no crime had technically been committed.

Civil rights groups and free speech activists often eyed our work with distrust. They argued that by monitoring recruiters, we were infringing on religious freedom and free speech. Back then, social media companies refused to censor online profiles unless they directly called for the violent overthrow of the U.S. or incited violence. We respected that stance, knowing it's not America's job to police unpopular ideas. The Supreme Court's "imminent threat" standard kept us from regulating even the most hateful speech. It wasn't until groups like ISIS and Al-Shabab were tagged as foreign terrorist organizations that we could bring criminal charges for recruitment or material support.

Jump to the present, and the stated goal of DHS's new board was to stop the "threat" of disinformation. The Secretary's repeated use of the word "threat" should concern us all. This language links disinformation to potential physical harm, making it easier to justify criminal investigations and prosecutions.

We already have laws for dealing with harmful false information. Civil penalties exist for defamation and slander, and criminal charges can be brought for perjury or obstructing justice. The Constitution doesn't let the government punish a story for being exaggerated or an opinion for being unorthodox. Look at the Hunter Biden laptop saga: initially dismissed as a fringe conspiracy, it was later proven true. The debates over masks and vaccines during COVID show us that ideas, once rejected, can later prove true. It's the power of free speech that lets us explore, challenge, and grow as new evidence emerges. This fundamental right has driven monumental changes like ending slavery and winning women's suffrage. It's through this spirited exchange of ideas that we make progress, shaping a more just and enlightened society.

The recent drive to criminalize "unpopular" speech was ignited by the backlash against the parental rights movement. What started with passionate parents, fueled by frustration, led to a few altercations that prompted the Justice Department to issue a memo about prosecuting the perceived "threat" to school officials. Soon after, the DHS released a National Terrorism Advisory, highlighting a heightened threat from disinformation introduced by both foreign and domestic actors. Consider the language of the bulletin very carefully:

> "These threat actors seek to exacerbate societal friction to sow discord and undermine public trust in government institutions to encourage unrest, which could potentially inspire acts of violence."

The alarming conclusion is this: our leading national security agency says the most significant domestic terrorism threat today is from people who share unpopular ideas with others, which could make them angry enough to commit a crime. To address this apparent threat, they created a board to advise the operational departments of DHS on who to investigate and possibly prosecute for these alleged crimes. How is the US government suddenly the arbiter of "truth" and defining social unrest and lack of public trust as a potential terrorism threat?

As if the unconstitutionality of regulating truth in the public square is not bad enough, the choice of who was to govern the Disinformation Board makes it obvious who was the intended target of this effort. Nina Jankowicz, a clearly left-leaning social activist, has already labeled opponents of CRT "disinformers" and considers gender-based harassment online to be a national security threat, equal to terrorism.

U.S. law enforcement power should never be partisan. We saw how damaging that was during the Russian collusion debacle when corruption in senior leadership tarnished the stellar reputation of the FBI. DHS and FBI officials are also never meant to be the thought police. We pride ourselves on that as Americans. Thankfully, many legislators are voicing their objections to this partisan attempt to silence opposition.

Marsha Blackburn from Tennessee wrote to DHS that the "federal government has no place interfering with the rights of all Americans to speak publicly about their political views… In fact, the Supreme Court has made it abundantly clear that this kind of 'core political speech' is 'the primary object of First Amendment protection.'" In a statement issued by ranking Senator Rob Portman, he says, "I do not believe that the United States government should turn the tools that we have used to assist our allies to counter foreign adversaries onto the American people."

It is no secret that the U.S. has directly engaged in "disinformation" campaigns in countries worldwide to defeat communism, totalitarianism, and, in many cases, terrorist recruitment. The American people should not tolerate its government now turning around to tell us what truth we can or should believe.

Christians, even those who try to remain "apolitical," must realize we will be the greatest casualty of this effort. Our truth about who Jesus Christ is as God incarnate and that life begins with conception can easily be weaponized against us when the judge does not believe in God's Word. Look at the underwhelming response by law enforcement as the radicals torch Christian nonprofits and harass conservative Supreme Court judges at their homes. Nothing is being done to stop those crimes as if their values or legal rights do not matter.

FORTY-SIX

Targeting Christians in the U.S.

"Fear not, for I am with you; Be not dismayed, for I am your God. I will strengthen you, Yes, I will help you, I will uphold you with My righteous right hand."

Another dangerous sign of Christians being the target of persecution is the U.S. government's financial support of organizations that intentionally vilify mainstream organizations like the Christian Broadcasting Network [CBN] and Fox News.

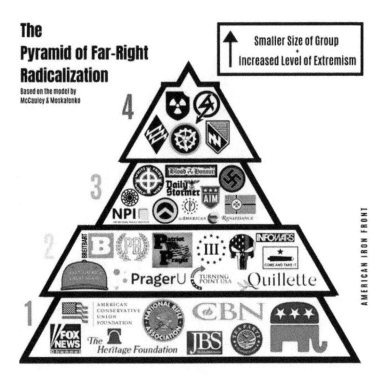

This graphic was used by one of the grantees of the Biden administration's Targeted Violence and Terrorism Prevention Grant Program [TVTP]. The program, titled differently but begun under Obama, was focused on the threat coming from terror groups like ISIS recruiting in the U.S. I was a recipient of several of those grants and was involved in many aspects of the programming that was developed during that time. We were tasked with developing innovative solutions to building resilience against radicalization. The program also funded research on effective intervention techniques and promoting social cohesion. The Trump administration reduced its funding, and Biden was poised to scrap it entirely because of complaints that it unfairly targeted Muslim and Arab communities.

However, in a dramatic turn, the Biden administration revamped the program to prioritize domestic violent extremism and targeted violence against communities of color. DHS Assistant Secretary John Cohen stated that it will focus on understanding the behaviors of those who engage in violence "directed at immigrant communities, communities of color, and different faith communities." This is vastly different from the original purpose of the grant program and the general understanding of terrorism in the U.S. for the past twenty years.

In 2022, the TVTP awarded 80 grants totaling just under $40 million. Based on the stated objectives of reducing what it calls domestic violent extremism, also referred to as "the alt-right," fascism, or white supremacy, many of the grantees are in "conservative" areas like the Miami Valley in Ohio.

To be clear, there is nothing wrong with investing federal funds to reduce targeted violence against immigrant communities. Promoting understanding, peace-building, and reconciliation are valuable principles for any society. However, this program in Ohio will only mainstream hate and division among its citizens.

Dr. Michael Loadenthal is the founder and executive director of the Prosecution Project. He presented on two different panels during the roundtable hosted by the TVTP grantee, the University of Dayton Human Rights Center. It is assumed that Loadenthal created the graphic in question since he used it in his presentation. He attributes his version of the pyramid to a model initially developed by Clark McCauley and Sophia Moskalenko, respected scholars in terrorism research. In their version, there are two different pyramids to distinguish groups prone to violent action from those only engaged in extremist opinions. It was purposely designed that way to acknowledge the overwhelming research findings that simply having "radical" ideologies does not create or lead to violent action. McCauley and Moskalenko did NOT insert these names in their models. In fact, they recently authored a vital research article on QAnon that passionately discourages the government from wasting resources on targeting such groups. Stated simply:

> "Trying to police opinion exaggerates the threat a hundredfold and wastes resources. Additionally, attempts to clamp down on radical opinions can backfire —by

creating real or perceived grievances in the targeted population, which can then radicalize people who would have otherwise remained neutral."[15]

Regardless of the lessons learned by focusing entirely on Muslims or the warnings sounded by scholars in the field of counterterrorism, this grantee completely disregarded the advice. In the video of his presentation entitled, "Anti-Fascist Intel in an Era Of Crowdsource Policing," Michael Loadenthal clearly defines his training goals for community members. He wants them to disrupt, de-platform, and prevent these groups from mobilizing or accessing the public square in person or online. He acknowledges that his methodology is sometimes illegal, especially their efforts to silence speech, but it does not matter to him. To Loadenthal, First Amendment rights do not extend to speech he does not like. Contrary to decades of terrorism research, he asserts that self-defined hate speech automatically mobilizes to violence and power, so it must be stopped at all costs.

Some tactics he deploys include training a citizen militia to troll their neighbors, co-workers, and friends for alt-right sympathizers and then report them to their employers, gyms, or churches so they can be fired or ostracized. He starts campaigns to pressure vendors like PayPal and Amazon not to let them raise donations or sell merchandise. He even had a graphic depicting how they led such a campaign against conservative pundit Steve Bannon. Loadenthal conflates conservative talk show hosts like Steven Bannon or TPUSA leader Charlie Kirk with Nazis and then teaches citizens to disrupt their livelihood.

The other speaker at the conference educated the audience on how to identify the alt-right in your local community by attending rallies. He described them as recruitment centers for radicalization, where the extremists get to interact and promote ideas. Can you imagine

---

[15] https://www.jstor.org/stable/pdf/27007300.pdf?refreqid=excelsior%3A52c7c526c09b47f07e6ed41d5f5eb63d&ab_segments=&origin=&initiator=&acceptTC=1

your neighbors finding out you went to a rally against drag shows in kindergarten and ending up losing your job because you're accused of being a Nazi?

The ideas presented by both these panelists, in the presence of a DHS official, were so shocking I encourage you to listen for yourself. It is incredibly alarming to know that millions of U.S. taxpayer funds may be used to scale and replicate this in cities across America. Encouraging citizens to report on each other and ruin their livelihood is right out of the playbook of a third-world dictatorship. How many of us have immigrant family members who tell horror stories about such things happening back in their home countries? Spending millions of U.S. taxpayer dollars to outsource policing can potentially rip apart our communities. That is not hyperbole; ask any Chinese or Russian immigrant what happens when the government turns its citizens against one another.

When I was personally involved in this field, entire programs could get scrapped if Muslim advocacy organizations complained that they were discriminatory. There were news articles exposing questionable practices, and grantees would be forced to adjust their methodology. Nonetheless, neither my colleagues nor I ever suggested the draconian methods advocated by these two participants. Stereotyping conservatives as fascists or Nazis without evidence of any wrongdoing will breed chaos, social strife, and unjust persecution. I could never imagine a similar graphic about Muslims being circulated as part of a federally funded program.

Furthermore, the U.S. government paid for research to evaluate the previous programs, which excessively stigmatized Muslims without yielding any positive outcomes. Despite the many criticisms, the government is using an even more extreme approach with the "alt-right," regardless of ample evidence that the methodology and principles are deeply flawed.

Surprisingly, there is very little public outcry about these programs. The Christian Broadcasting Network is being lumped together with the KKK, and only conservative commentators are reporting on it. There is no demand by mainstream Christian organizations or the mainstream media to review the Dayton program and others for unconstitutional and inappropriate practices.

The Preventing Radicalization to Extremist Violence Through Education, Network-Building, and Training in Southwest Ohio (PREVENTS-OH) claims its "mission is to work to address systemic injustice and promote peace, dignity, and human rights." Targeting and denigrating the residents of Miami Valley will never achieve peace and dignity.

It is important to note that the intention of the homeland security apparatus created after 9-11 was to prevent foreign-led terrorism perpetuated against U.S. interests. Whether U.S. soldiers fought overseas to capture or kill known terrorists or prevention programs were put in place in the U.S., the underlying principle was stopping foreign recruitment of Americans for terrorist attacks against U.S. interests, either domestic or overseas. Mechanisms like the Foreign Intelligence Surveillance Court provide investigatory powers to the government against foreign threats and are without defense counsel review to protect top-secret national security information. It was never intended that these programs would be used to stop the constitutionally protected activities of Americans. It is very problematic when counter-terrorism resources are repurposed to crush American political opponents.

Throughout my career, I was very involved in building many of the security programs now being weaponized against conservatives, so this whole situation is deeply personal. I recall meetings with representatives from social media giants like Google and Facebook, where we pleaded with them to remove the accounts of suspected foreign terror recruiters. At the time, they were extremely hesitant about interfering in the free speech arena. They were uncomfortable about making a judgment call on who was a potential terrorist. They did not want to be seen as an arm of the U.S. government, yet over time, their attitude clearly changed. Now, these same social media giants close the accounts of anyone they ideologically disagree with. Consequently, supporters of international terrorism, like members of the Iranian government, have an unfettered ability to post online. But people who support the right to life, oppose forced vaccines, or, dare I say, are Trump supporters, get regularly banned or suspended.

I remember how libertarians used to warn against the overreach of law enforcement caused by the new clandestine national security network and the potential for abuse. Many of us experts didn't believe them, but now we see that danger coming to pass. The perilous consequence of this abuse of power is dividing our country. Remember, Americans are an armed population. The Second Amendment guarantees the right to bear and possess firearms. Wrongfully accusing, harassing, and imprisoning a large segment of American society for their beliefs can potentially create a very bloody conflict. Frankly, there's no calculable end to what can happen.

Though the enemy used to be just foreign actors intent to harm Americans, the new public enemy appears to be American conservatives and people who hold Biblical values. Let's hope Congressional leaders will come together and investigate the miscarriages of justice and the erosion of our constitutionally protected right to religious freedom, free speech, and political opposition.

For believers, though there are dark days ahead of us, we must always remember that our trust and our hope are never in earthly things. Our faith and trust are only in our God, our Lord and Savior, Jesus Christ. We are invincible until God calls us home. We all have an expiration date, and we won't live one minute more or less. That surety in God and His protection should be a great source of comfort, regardless of what happens in the world around us.

FORTY-SEVEN

Government Overreach Against "Radical" Catholics

In another stunning revelation about government overreach, a whistleblower exposed an internal FBI memo identifying *Radical Traditional Catholicism* [RTC] as a potential breeding ground for terrorists or what they call *Racially Motivated Violent Extremists* [RMVE]. By way of background, the government's definition of a "violent extremist" is the following:

> "U.S.-based actors who conduct or threaten activities that are dangerous to human life in violation of the criminal laws... intended to intimidate or coerce a civilian population, and influence the policy of a government... by mass destruction, assassination, or kidnapping..."

I know firsthand that the government decided on the expression "violent extremist" to avoid associating the religion of Islam with terrorism. It was also helpful because it was broad enough to encompass those who committed ideologically motivated violence for many other reasons, including racial superiority or the protection of animal rights. In the field of counter-terrorism, it is grossly inappropriate to directly associate an entire religious group with violence because a single member or group of individuals engage in criminal behavior. The FBI, in particular, has a legal prohibition against targeting individuals based on religious beliefs. This memo includes a warning to that effect:

> "Potential criminality by certain members of a group referenced herein does not negate ...the constitutional rights of the group itself or its members. The FBI does not investigate, collect or maintain information on U.S. persons solely for the purpose of monitoring activities protected by the First Amendment."

Despite the warning, this FBI analyst provides an inflammatory definition of Radical Traditional Catholic doctrine to supposedly educate the reader about why its members are potentially dangerous. *"RTCs are typically characterized by a rejection of the Vatican II; disdain for most of the popes elected since...and frequent adherence to anti-Semitic, anti-immigrant, anti-LGBTQ and white supremacist ideology."* Citations include several left-leaning news articles and the often-biased research of the Southern Poverty Law Center. There is no evidence that this religious group has committed a single act of violence. The author also acknowledges this memo is the first to identify the RTCs as a threat. The accusations made in this document were so alarming I looked up the organizations and doctrine for myself.

As a disclaimer, I have no personal knowledge or experience with the divisions in the Catholic church and its doctrine. However, I did spend most of my professional career researching ideologically motivated violence. I can recognize when a group uses inflammatory language to incite followers into criminal behavior. After reading and listening to several of the groups listed in the memo, it is shocking that the FBI legal counsel approved this document as credible. To summarize, most groups dubbed "RTCs" are upset with how Vatican II abolished many of the ancient practices that survived for centuries. They felt like subsequent Catholic leadership was throwing away long-held traditions, which included a Latin mass. They see it as a breakdown of the traditional Catholic values on everything from gender relations to sexual promiscuity and even abortions. Another theme amongst these "RTC" groups is a rejection of the post-Vatican II movement towards ecumenicalism, which claims all religions are equal and worship the same God. It fails to acknowledge the primacy of Jesus Christ for salvation or His Lordship. Many of the debates between Catholic scholars on the future direction of the church sound very similar to the ones we have in mainstream churches across America. The concern over corrupt cultural norms seeping into the church is happening everywhere, regardless of denomination.

One organization posted content about the historical conflict between Judaism and Catholicism to justify their objection to improved relations between the two communities. Their reasoning stems from the crucifixion of Jesus and the subsequent persecution of the church. It is a religious conflict that dates back 2000 years. As despicable as these ideas may be, the groups did NOT advocate violence whatsoever and made no association with being white or with racially motivated groups like the KKK. In fact, white nationalist groups historically despise Catholics as much as they do Jews or Blacks, so associating these two movements together is a ridiculous hypothesis. Furthermore, to claim that a traditional Catholic's opposition to liberalism means that a person is an antisemite is a gross misstatement of the ideas and principles behind conventional Catholicism.

Thankfully, 20 attorney generals from around the country wrote a scathing letter to the DOJ and FBI condemning the unconstitutionality of the focus on one religious community based on its beliefs and the suggestion to cultivate spies inside the Catholic church who can report on their activities. Though the FBI claims it has retracted the memo, the letter dismisses that action as simply a ruse to cover up its already committed malfeasance. The signatories demanded accountability to ensure the Catholic community was not persecuted or subject to bias and hostility within the FBI.

It is important for all Americans, especially the church, to realize that everyone is a potential target once the government starts characterizing deeply held religious beliefs as the impetus for violence. Many people dismissed the overly aggressive targeting of January 6 attendees because it was associated with Trump, whom they already disliked. However, this memo demonstrates that if our government decides to investigate a group of people based on their "unpopular" beliefs, all Bible-believing Christians may be in danger one day. Americans take pride in protecting religious liberty as the cornerstone of our society. It is abhorrent for any branch of the U.S. government to behave contrary to that principle.

— FORTY-EIGHT —

The Left's Gender Jihad
Against Christians

When both mainstream media and the government elevate the hatred and vilification of Christian ideals, the result is everyday citizens who wreak havoc in society. This was in full display when a deranged young trans female gunned down three small children and three adults in cold blood at a small church school in Nashville. The killer had a carefully laid out plan to murder as many people as possible to further her social-political goals. According to the FBI definition, this was clearly an act of domestic terrorism. Yet, strangely enough, the media and the White House scrambled to vindicate the perpetrator rather than call attention to the ideological extremism that underpins this violence.

The shooter's exact motives, as described in her manifesto, were recently released to the public, which confirmed that she planned for months to commit mass murder at the Christian school. Several commentators point to the recent surge of what some call "anti-trans" legislation, including those passed in Tennessee, which could have inflamed the sentiments of this troubled young woman. There was also some discussion about how she resented being sent to the Christian school as a child.

As is customary in the U.S., after a terrorist attack, the focus of the media and public officials immediately turned to gun legislation. A futile discussion that enrages both sides of the political aisle—the ban on assault rifles—will never solve the underlying problems that lead people to murder. Conservative pundits point out the surprising pattern that Aubre Hale is the fourth in a string of mass casualty attacks perpetuated by people who identified as trans or non-binary. Rather than calling national attention to why this phenomenon is occurring, the White House scrambled to declare "Trans Visibility Day" just days after the shooting. The Press Secretary, Karine Jean-Pierre, denounced the "anti-trans" bills that "attack trans kids and their families" as if to imply that trans violence is justified as self-defense. They are being rewarded with permanent victim status by the left. In fact, President Biden laughed when asked if this was a hate crime, saying, "No, I don't have any idea."

There is a blatant disregard for the status of the victims or the fear in the hearts of Christian families who now worry if they will be the targets of additional attacks. Consider what other movement could get away with plotting a "Day of Vengeance"? This language is acceptable to them because they feel entitled to affirmation and submission from the wider society. The media and government support their cause of retaliation because it is directed at a common enemy: those rebel conservatives. It is the Bible-thumping bigots who are the problem. This is clearly a movement of hate, not liberation or freedom.

Our constitutional order holds that we are equal under the law because we are all created in God's image. This essential insight is precisely what transgender ideology is determined to undermine. They claim mankind can "make" itself into whatever fashion it deems fit. Anyone who disagrees with this premise must be forced into submission, isolation, and now even death. It's not enough for them to insist on the legal right to castrate their children and expose them to pornographic content in kindergarten; everyone is forced to accept it or face grave consequences. We also should realize that transgenderism is an extremely lucrative industry. Corporate elites in the pharmaceutical and medical industry, including major political donors, are all profiting from the despair of others.

This demonic ideology claims dominion over man's divine status, which Christians can never accept. However, we certainly do not use it to justify physical violence.

> *"See that no one repays another with evil for evil, but always seek after that which is good for one another and for all people."*
>
> *—1 Thessalonians 5:15*

Instead, Christians advocate for laws to ban gender reassignment in minors because we want to protect *all* children from making decisions they could regret once they mature into rational adults. The facts about gender dysphoria, which psychiatric professionals classify as "gender identity disorder," validate this approach. The study published in 2020 by the Journal of Psychiatry Treatment and Research states:

> "The psychiatric comorbidity [presence of two or more diseases] in these patients shows shocking figures. Some studies demonstrate that 40-45% of *trans* adolescents have psychiatric comorbidity...the most frequent are depression, anxiety, self-harm episodes, and suicide attempts... Furthermore, other studies suggest that up to *80% of transgender children and adolescents* seem to give up, or in other words, they try to identify as cisgender when reaching an older age."[16]

Allowing children to physically mutilate themselves is irresponsible and cruel, knowing that 80% of them grow out of it.

---

[16] https://scholars.direct/Articles/psychiatry/jptr-3-007.php?jid=psychiatry

Later, as an adult, if the dysphoria continues, they have the legal freedom to undergo gender transition. It is their free will to choose. Christians are not transphobic. We do not hate those who live in contravention to God, but we have a deep-seated desire to prevent harm. As Christ's followers, we despise the sin, not the sinner. We pray for each and every one of them to come to a saving faith that will free them from the bondage of sin and death. However, there is no compulsion.

> *"This day I call the heavens and the earth as witnesses against you that I have set before you life and death, blessings and curses. Now choose life so that you and your children may live and that you may love the* LORD *your God, listen to His voice, and hold fast to Him."*
>
> *—Deuteronomy 30:19-20*

Over the past several years, the Biden administration and the media have recharacterized the passion of parents, Catholics, and conservatives to protect children as the greatest threat to America and democracy. Yet none of these groups is gunning down innocent people. The true face of domestic terrorism is the deceived followers of the radical left agenda.

FORTY-NINE

God's Heart for Israel

"Who has ever seen anything as strange as this? Who ever heard of such a thing? Has a nation ever been born in a single day? Has a country ever come forth in a mere moment? But by the time Jerusalem's birth pains begin, her children will be born."

—*Isaiah 66:8 NLT*

The focus of the Abraham Accords was normalizing Israeli relations with its Arab neighbors. A key draw for these countries was creating a robust U.S.-backed partnership against the threat of Iran's nuclearization and its continued support of terrorism worldwide. However, many other benefits developed from the treaty, and standing firm against Tehran was one of the primary motivations. The diplomatic ties and strategic partnerships that ensued finally exposed as a lie the longstanding premise that no peace could be possible in the Middle East without resolving the Israeli-Palestinian conflict.

Though the Abraham Accords created great hope for the future of peace between Israel and its Middle East neighbors, those efforts were dramatically and brutally destroyed by the HAMAS massacre.

On October 7, 2023, coordinated armed attacks were launched from the Gaza Strip into southern Israel. It was the first invasion of Israeli territory since the 1948 Arab-Israeli War. The assault coincided with the Jewish holiday of Simchat Torah. HAMAS and other Palestinian militant groups called the operation "Operation Al-Aqsa Flood," while in Israel it is known as Black Saturday. Internationally, it is referred to as the October 7 attacks. This event triggered the ongoing Israel-HAMAS war.

The attacks began with at least 4,300 rockets fired into Israel, accompanied by incursions via vehicles and powered paragliders. HAMAS fighters breached the Gaza-Israel barrier, targeting military bases and attacking civilians in 21 communities. According to an IDF report, approximately 6,000 militants from Gaza breached the border at 119 points, including 3,800 elite Nukhba forces and 2,200 other militants and civilians. Additionally, around 1,000 Gazans were involved in firing rockets, bringing the total number of attackers to around 7,000.

The attacks resulted in the brutal slaughter of 1,139 people, including 695 Israeli civilians (among them 38 children), 71 foreign nationals, and 373 security personnel. At the Nova music festival alone, 364 civilians were killed, and many others were wounded. About 250 Israeli civilians and soldiers, including 30 children, were taken hostage to Gaza, either dead or alive, to pressure Israel to exchange them for Palestinian prisoners. Reports also indicated cases of vicious rape and sexual assault.

Worldwide public opinion was in support of Israel, but the sympathy dramatically shifted and erupted into a new wave of antisemitism throughout the U.S. and Europe. This has also bled over into the Christian community, with popular conservative influencers denouncing U.S. support for Israel.

What most people do not realize about Islamist terrorists like HAMAS is that they launch countless rockets indiscriminately into civilian areas and send their women and children into the line of fire as a tactic to garner public support for their cause. They have taken billions of dollars in international aid and bought palaces for their officials while their people die in poverty. They take the money to build underground tunnels rather than building societal infrastructure.

The tragic loss of life in this conflict cannot be overstated. Each new U.S. administration and nearly every international body repeatedly attempts to broker a political solution but to no avail. When it comes to HAMAS, like other designated terrorist groups, their embrace of radical Islam makes a political solution impossible.

I can assure you there are thousands of sincere Muslims who condemn terrorism and politically motivated violence. Yet, what started as a small sect of extremists is now a complex transnational network of organizations and individuals working for almost a century to use religion as a weapon of war. Though some focus regionally, like HAMAS, and others like Al-Qaeda, are global, all these factions interpret Islam in a way that justifies the killing of innocent civilians to establish their social and political goals. As an example, the military wing of HAMAS known as Qassam Brigades used to have on their website:

> "There is no doubt that suicide operations in the way of god, against the enemies of God and his messenger, and the enemies of the Muslims, are a noble act of worship which bring the Muslim closer to his lord."

For Americans, the conflict in the Middle East may seem like an endless quagmire of competing interests that we are rarely in a position to change. However, Christians must understand God's heart for Israel and its people. From the beginning, God promises to Abraham:

> *I will make you into a great nation and I will bless you; I will make your name great, and you will be a blessing. I will bless*

those who bless you, and whoever curses you I will curse, and all peoples on earth will be blessed through you."

—Genesis 12:2-3

This is a promise for all believers that blessings come to those who bless Israel.

We are also told that it is God Himself who established its boundaries. Before Joshua enters the promised land, God decrees:

"Every place on which the sole of your foot treads, I have given it to you, just as I spoke to Moses. From the wilderness and this Lebanon, even as far as the great river, the river Euphrates, all the land of the Hittites, and as far as the Great Sea toward the setting of the sun will be your territory."

—Joshua 1: 3-4

Though the Israelites repeatedly disobeyed God's commandments and were often punished for their transgressions, His commitment to them never changed because the character and nature of God are irreversible. Throughout the Bible, culminating in the final restoration of the nation of Israel in the book of Revelation, God decries the destruction and divisions of its territory while repeatedly swearing an oath to avenge its people.

"In those days and at that time, when I restore the fortunes of Judah and Jerusalem, I will gather all nations and bring them down to the Valley of Jehoshaphat. There I will put them on trial for what they did to my inheritance, my people Israel, because they scattered my people among the nations and divided up my land... The Lord will roar from Zion and thunder from Jerusalem; the earth and the heavens will tremble. But the Lord will be a refuge for His people, a stronghold for the people of Israel."

—Joel 3:1-21, 6-17

So, despite what governments will do in response to a political or social crisis, as believers, we must acknowledge that God's heart for Israel is not to divide its land or oppress its people. As a former Muslim, the love for Israel and its people is an entirely new experience for me, but I am grateful the Lord has opened my heart to this understanding. Any nation or people that defy these principles makes itself liable to the judgment of God for its actions in contradiction to His will.

The future of Israel and its ultimate restoration, as outlined in Biblical prophecy, gives believers a profound sense of hope and purpose. The Scriptures reassure us that despite the trials and tribulations Israel may face, the Lord remains unwavering in His covenant. This divine fidelity underscores the importance of steadfast faith and adherence to God's grand design. As believers, our role is to align our lives and actions with God's vision, exemplifying faith through our endeavors and interactions.

As everyday Christians, our mission extends beyond prayer and encompasses active engagement in spreading the Gospel. This includes sharing the transformative message of Christ with both Jews and Muslims. The salvation of the Jewish people and the peaceful conversion of Muslims, who may often find themselves trapped in cycles of anger and vengeance, are pivotal to realizing the divine prophecy. We believe that the love and grace of Christ offers a path to healing and redemption, no matter one's past. The story of people like Mosab Yousef[17], the son of a HAMAS founder who converted to Christianity, is a testament to the profound change Christ's saving grace can bring.

An open heart, willing to embrace the transformative power of faith in Jesus as Lord and Savior, holds the key to shifting the paradigm in the Middle East from conflict to reconciliation. It's through this profound personal transformation that the region can move from a place of darkness to light, from hatred to love, and from

---

[17] https://www.amazon.com/Son-Hamas-Gripping-Political-Unthinkable/dp/1414333080

devastation to peace. Each individual who turns to Christ contributes to this larger divine plan, fostering a community rooted in the love and teachings of Jesus. Indeed, it is through such conversions and the spreading of the Gospel that we can hope to witness a tangible shift toward peace and divine fulfillment in the Middle East.

ABOUT THE AUTHOR

Hedieh Mirahmadi Falco brings a wealth of experience from her dynamic career in national security to her latest venture as an author. With over two decades dedicated to serving in various capacities, including as a political officer in the U.S. Embassy in Afghanistan and a senior advisor to FBI Headquarters, Hedieh has tirelessly worked to mitigate threats of mass targeted violence while fostering better relationships between communities and law enforcement.

After a notable career, Hedieh discovered a newfound passion for sharing the Gospel of Jesus Christ. She now dedicates her life to evangelical missions. Her main focus is the *ResurrectMinistry.com* platform, which enables global access to salvation. Additionally, Hedieh serves as an exclusive columnist for *The Christian Post* and co-hosts the *Living Fearless Devotional* daily podcast with her husband, where they provide insightful discussions on faith and life.

Hedieh's expertise has garnered attention from major media outlets such as CNN, CBS News, C-SPAN, and Fox News. She has also authored numerous articles addressing the challenges of countering the Islamist threat in the U.S. and continues to engage in public discourse through radio interviews and podcasts.

With a Juris Doctor from the University of Southern California Law School and an undergraduate degree in history from the University of California, Los Angeles, Hedieh blends her legal, analytical, and business acumen with her fervent commitment to spreading the message of hope and redemption found in Christ.

www.ingramcontent.com/pod-product-compliance
Lightning Source LLC
Chambersburg PA
CBHW052314040525
26167CB00011B/878